At Issue

| Organ Transplants

Other books in the At Issue series:

At Issue

Organ Transplants

Susan C. Hunnicutt, Book Editor

GREENHAVEN PRESS

An imprint of Thomson Gale, a part of The Thomson Corporation

Detroit • New York • San Francisco • New Haven, Conn. • Waterville, Maine • London

Christine Nasso, *Publisher*
Elizabeth Des Chenes, *Managing Editor*

© 2007 The Gale Group.

For more information, contact:
Greenhaven Press
27500 Drake Rd.
Farmington Hills, MI 48331-3535
Or you can visit our Internet site at http://www.gale.com

LIBRARY OF CONGRESS CATALOGING-IN-PUBLICATION DATA

Organ Transplants / Susan C. Hunnicutt, book editor.
    p. cm. -- (At issue)
  Includes bibliographical references and index.
  ISBN-13: 978-0-7377-3691-5 (hardcover)
  ISBN-13: 978-0-7377-3692-2 (pbk.)
  1. Transplantation of organs, tissues, etc.--Juvenile literature. I. Hunnicutt, Susan.
  RD120.76.O74 2008
  617.9'5--dc22

                                                                    2007026032

ISBN-10: 0-7377-3691-7 (hardcover)
ISBN-10: 0-7377-3692-5 (pbk.)

Printed in the United States of America
10 9 8 7 6 5 4 3 2 1

Contents

Introduction

Advances in medical technology have produced a growing demand for life-saving organ transplants. That human organs should be treated as commodities that can be bought and sold is a suggestion that is being made with increasing frequency. "World markets match buyers and sellers for goods as different as oil and wheat or cars and computers. Why not for human organs like kidneys?" asks Tom Heneghan in an April 3, 2007, Reuters article about a European conference on organ transplantation policy.

In the United States, most organs used for transplant surgery are harvested shortly after death, from individuals who have died in accidents. The United Network for Organ Sharing, under contract with the federal government, maintains a waiting list for scarce organs and serves as a clearinghouse, matching organs with recipients awaiting transplant surgery. In the United States, the exchange of money for organs is illegal. Families of deceased donors are not even allowed to accept money to pay for funeral expenses.

However, in some parts of the developing world, the ability to successfully remove a kidney from a living donor for transplant into another person has led to a phenomenon called "transplant tourism," in which wealthy patients travel abroad for needed surgeries, purchasing organs from living donors, presumably impoverished, who choose to give up an organ in exchange for cash. Individuals in countries such as India, Pakistan, Iraq, and Turkey might receive the equivalent of from $500 to $5,000 dollars in exchange for one of their kidneys.

Transplant tourism is becoming more prevalent in developing nations because of a growing gap between the numbers of people in need of organs and the numbers of available donors. In the United States alone, in 2005, more than 28,000 solid organ transplants—kidney, liver, lung, heart, pancreas, and intestine—were performed. During the same period the number of patients on waiting lists for organs in the United States was approaching 90,000. The most hotly debated issue in the organ transplant community today is how to close this gap, to procure enough organs to meet the burgeoning need.

In 2006, the Institute of Medicine (IOM), part of the National Academy of Sciences, released a report titled *Organ Donation: Opportunities for Action*, that addressed the organ shortage. The report suggested first that hospitals and other medical institutions could improve donation rates by working to integrate the opportunity for organ donation into routine care for dying patients. "Patients and their families should be offered the opportunity to donate as standard end-of-life care, and information on organ donation processes should be an integral part of the many other decisions that are faced at this time," the report said.

Second, the report recommended fine-tuning procedures for obtaining consent for organ donation in cases where the determination of death is made according to circulatory, rather than neurological criteria. This is a complex medical distinction. In many cases where death is pronounced because the heart has stopped beating, the decision to donate is frequently delayed by a potential conflict of interest between donor, recipient, and physician. By the time death can be established according to neurological criteria—the determination that brain death has occurred—it is too late to harvest the organs (organs for donation must be removed very shortly after death if they are to be usable). The IOM report advocates research to fine-tune medical response in this kind of circumstance to assure that the rights of potential donors are protected in a way that still allows the donation of healthy organs when death does occur.

Third, the report recommends that the transplant community work to change the social climate through education to address people's fears about organ donation and, ultimately, to create a society where people see organ donation as "a social responsibility" and "a normal part of dying." Attitude change through education is preferable to any kind of legislation that would mandate that a choice be made or that would establish presumed consent as the rule in cases of sudden death.

In addition to these measures to increase the supply of healthy organs available for transplant, the Institute of Medicine supports the present policy in the United States that organ donation must always be an act of giving, without financial compensation of any kind either for the organ itself or, for example, to pay funeral expenses. However, this position has drawn sharp criticism in some quarters. Richard Epstein, writing for the *Wall Street Journal* in May of 2006, called the IOM report "a dreadful disappointment . . . narrowminded and unimaginative," because of its failure to endorse market incentives—the exchange of cash—as a way of increasing the numbers of donated organs. Citing the dire circumstances of the 6,000 persons each year who are added to organ waiting lists, Epstein wrote, "There is little room for upward movement . . . without fundamental change. The welcome decline in traumatic deaths has cut back on the supply of cadaveric organs. Yet while many individuals will give to family members and some will donate even to strangers, the truth remains the supply of live organ donors available at no cost will lag far behind the demand." Epstein bases his argument on simple economic theory: that increasing the price that will be paid organ donors or their families will lead to an increase in the supply of available organs. The IOM report, however, rejects the suggestion that organs should be treated like other commodities available in a market economy. It cites the concern that financial remuneration for organs "might disproportionately affect the poor or other marginalized groups, and might also cause a drop in donations for altruistic purposes."

While most medical procedures involve only two individuals, the doctor and the patient, the transplant of human organs necessarily involves a third party—the donor who provides the life-giving organ. The issue of how to meet the needs of a person who is ill in a timely and compassionate way, while respecting the rights and the personhood of this third party, who is equally in need of just and compassionate care, lies at the center of many of the viewpoints that are presented in *At Issue: Organ Transplants.*

1

The Urgent Need for Donor Organs Raises Complex Ethical Questions

President's Council on Bioethics

The President's Council on Bioethics advises the president of the United States on bioethical issues that may emerge as a consequence of advances in biomedical science and technology.

The ability to treat disease by transplanting human organs has resulted in many lives saved and in improved quality of life for many individuals suffering from chronic illnesses. At the same time, the resulting demand for organs raises complex and often troubling ethical questions. Differing perspectives on the dignity and integrity of the human body and the limits and obligations of the medical profession must be taken into account in developing public policy to encourage organ donation and to regulate organ donation practices. The following paper was prepared to aid the President's Council in its decisions about policy options in organ procurement, transplantation, and allocation. It was designed to facilitate and inform Council discussions and does not represent the official views of the Council or of the U.S. government.

Since the first human kidney was transplanted in 1954, the nation has engaged in searching public discussions about the ethics of organ transplantation: about the human significance of removing organs from both living and cadaveric do-

"President's Council on Bioethics," *Staff Background Paper*, January, 2003. Reproduced by permission.

nors; about the criteria for determining when death occurs and thus when the decedent's organs might be taken; about whose wishes should ultimately decide whether organs are used or not used; and about the ethics of different organ procurement and allocation laws.

The current organ policy is shaped largely by two important laws: The first is the Uniform Anatomical Gift Act of 1968, adopted in all fifty states, which granted individuals the right to decide before death whether they wished to donate their organs; the second is the Organ Transplantation Act of 1984, which aimed to encourage organ donation by establishing an organized organ matching and procurement network, while outlawing the buying and selling of human organs or the direct compensation of organ donors and their families. Taken together, these laws sought to reap the medical benefits of organ transplantation and to encourage individuals to become organ donors, while preserving certain ethical limits against treating the body as property and the newly dead as simply natural resources. It also sought to ensure, as much as possible given other inequities in the health-care system, that organs are allocated in an equitable way.

Before considering the moral arguments for and against different organ procurement policies, one must first consider the human context and human meaning of organ transplantation itself.

Many Changes Have Been Considered

Whether this policy has been a great success or terrible failure—both medically and ethically—is a complex question. Many lives have been saved that would not have been otherwise, and yet waiting lists for organs continue to increase. Many individuals have given of themselves (literally) to save the life of another, and yet the unequivocal protection of those who are not-yet-dead (but would be useful if they were) has been called into question. The human body (dead or alive) has not been reduced to mere property, and yet the desperation of watching thousands of individuals die every year while waiting for organs has prompted a renewed debate about whether monetary incentives should be used in an effort to increase organ supply.

In the 107th Congress (2001–2002), a number of bills aimed at promoting organ donation and increasing organ supply were proposed. Some bills would have provided formal recognition of donors with commemorative medals. Other bills offered tax credits to individuals who donate organs (or credits to their surviving families) or reimbursement of the costs incurred by living donors. In addition, numerous books and articles have been written claiming that the current organ procurement system has been a failure, resulting in "prolonged suffering, declining health, and rising death rates," [according to Kaserman and Barnett, 2002] and that the time has come to explore a market-based system to solve the organ supply problem. A new group—called LifeSharers—is attempting to develop a private network of organ giving and receiving, so that members have first priority on the organs of other members. And while the medical community generally supports the guiding principle of the current policy—that organ donation should be an act of giving, without monetary incentives of any kind—the American Society of Transplant Surgeons has endorsed the idea of a pilot program that would partially reimburse surviving families for the funeral expenses of individuals who allow their organs to be taken after death.

The Human Context for Considering Organ Transplantation

Before considering the moral arguments for and against different organ procurement policies, one must first consider the human context and human meaning of organ transplantation itself. This context is first of all the dignity and integrity of the human body. A frequent line of argument in the organ transplantation debate is that organs are "no use" to individuals after they have died. No doubt this is in a certain sense true. And yet, it suggests that an individual's body has meaning only because it is "useful"; that the body is a tool individuals have rather than what individuals *are*. We are tempted, as Gilbert Meilaender has written, "to suppose that the 'real' person transcends the body." But in fact, our humanity and identity are inseparable from our bodies—including the human *dilemmas* that arise when our bodies fail us, the *humor* we experience when bodies sometimes have a mind of their own, the *grace* or *excellence* that we embody when we (our bodies) perform in ways only we (they) can, and the *dignity* of fundamental human-bodily activities such as the loving embrace and procreation.

Of course, modern medicine and medical progress depend on gaining some mastery of the body, including the routine study of the dead so that we might gain knowledge to help the living, and experimentation on living individuals' bodies in the hope of curing dreaded diseases. Medicine often involves "violating" the body in order to "save" it—for example, amputating a limb or opening the chest to operate on the heart. In the case of organ transplantation, this "violation" is done to one person, living or dead, in order to save another—with possibilities both for great *charity* and great *coercion* that this intervention entails.

The Obligations and Limits of Medicine

This brings us to the second context for understanding organ transplantation: the obligations and limits of medicine. No one can deny the great good that has come from organ transplantation in both lives saved and suffering ameliorated, as well as the great suffering that cannot be ameliorated because of the organ shortage. And yet, if saving the most possible lives while inflicting the least harm on the living were the only significant human obligation, then our policy on organ transplantation (not to mention human experimentation) would be very different. Society could simply take all available organs, and treat dead bodies as a public resource. But we do not do this, and for good reason. The obligation to heal—as fundamental as it is to the good life and good society—exists in concert (and sometimes in conflict) with other human values: the principle of autonomy, the duty of families to mourn the deceased, the responsibility of doctors to do no harm even when very great good might come from it.

Whose wishes should finally prevail in determining whether organs are taken—the dead person himself while he or she was living or the family that must mourn the deceased after death?

Beyond this, there are many further questions to consider: Whose wishes should finally prevail in determining whether organs are taken—the dead person himself while he or she was living or the family that must mourn the deceased after death? Does autonomy mean having the right to dispose of one's body (or enter into contracts for one's body) in any way an individual sees fit? Do fears about turning the body into property justify policies—such as no payment for organs—that potentially limit the supply of a life-saving "resource" and limit the right of individuals to make decisions about their bodies before and after death? Are there legitimate moral reasons *not* to be an organ donor or not to allow the organs of a deceased loved one to be taken? Do siblings or parents, while alive, have a moral obligation to donate organs to siblings or children who would otherwise die? Has the possibility of organ transplantation created new kinds of pressures or new forms of suffering—such as waiting in misery on organ waiting lists, and perhaps facing a death that comes to seem "unnecessary"?

Organ Transplantation and Public Policy

With these difficult questions in mind, we now turn to consider a number of different systems for governing the procurement of cadaveric organs. We begin with three caveats: First, it is impossible to separate the ethical-political debate over cadaveric organs from the debate over living organ donation: many of the principles involved (such as the meaning of treating the body as property) and the practical dilemmas (such as the problem of rationing an insufficient supply of organs or deciding whether or not to donate) overlap. Second, it is not easy in practice—though possible in principle—to separate the debate over organ procurement (how we get organs) from the debate over organ allocation (how we distribute them): for one thing, people's moral assessment of how organs are allocated might affect their judgment about whether to become organ donors, and proposals to compensate individuals for providing organs potentially entail their right to sell their organs to the highest bidder. Third, many proposed policies—especially organ compensation and organ markets—are untested hypotheses; this means that their claims can neither be written off in advance nor accepted at face value. One of the most important questions in this debate is why some people or some families decide not to donate their organs, and thus whether or not payment would change this behavior.

To think about public policy in this area means balancing these different realities and facing soberly the moral costs and benefits of different policies.

William F. May has described the different principles that might govern an organ procurement system as "giving-and-receiving" (the current system of altruistic organ donation), "taking-and-getting" (a system of routine retrieval of all organs without the explicit consent of the deceased or the surviving family), and "selling-and-buying" (a system of organ markets). One might add two others to this list: "honoring-and-shaming" (a system of public medals and community pressure) and "compensating-and-providing" (a system of public payment or tax credits for organ "donors"). We must, as we judge these different policies, think about the meaning of organ transplantation in its fullness: that is, about *organ donation* as a "gift of life," *organ retrieval* as a violation of the human body, *organ transplantation* as a "noble form of cannibalism," and the *organ shortage* as a tragedy for those individuals and families that wait for organs and often die waiting. To think about public policy in this area means balancing these different realities and facing soberly the moral costs and benefits of different policies.

Three Unacceptable Policies

We begin by considering three policies—what we might call ideal types in reverse—that nearly all Americans would rightfully find unacceptable for different reasons; understanding why these policies are unacceptable can perhaps guide us as we seek to discern the most responsible and prudent policy. The first is a policy of *organ conscription* or mandatory organ retrieval. Under such a policy, all cadaver organs would be retrieved regardless of the wishes of the deceased individual or the surviving family; dead bodies would be treated simply as a public resource in the service of the common goal of saving human life. The second is a policy of *unrestricted autonomy*, which would allow individuals, dead or alive, to enter into any contracts they wish for the buying-and-selling of their organs. The guiding principle of such a policy is that individuals "own" their bodies as a "possession," and that only individuals can weigh the risks versus benefits, the pains versus pleasures, entailed in deciding whether to keep, sell, or be buried with one's organs. Such a policy would include, on its own principles, the right to sell vital organs while alive (so-called "lethal transplants"), since an individual might rationally decide that the satisfaction of providing money for his family out-weighs his desire to continue living. (And his family might agree!) The third policy is *state-mandated protection of the inviolability of all bodies*, dead or alive. Such a policy would outlaw all organ retrieval, on the principle that the body ought not to be turned into a thing, even for a noble purpose such as saving life and that the activity of mourning must not be interfered with by removing the deceased individual's organs.

Each of these policies, by trying to preserve or pursue an absolute but isolated human good—saving the most life, granting the largest possible measure of individual autonomy, protecting the integrity of bodily life—ends up compromising or sacrificing other vital human goods. By seeing the error of these policies, we are perhaps awakened to the challenge of making a policy (or preserving the existing policy) that is both more moderate and more sober. . . .

Organ Donation ("Giving and Receiving"):

Under the current system, individuals can decide before death whether they wish to donate their organs after they die. As a legal matter, this positive decision to be an organ donor gives the surviving family no say; in practice, however, the surviving kin are typically asked permission, and in cases when families of organ donors do not wish for the decedent's organs to be taken, those family wishes are typically respected. In cases where individuals have made no declaration positively or negatively about whether they wished their organs to be removed, the decision is left to the surviving family entirely.

The guiding principles of this system, as described above, are the following: to encourage organ donation; to respect, as much as possible, both the prior wishes of the individual who has died and the wishes of the surviving family; to prevent the commodification of the body or perverse incentives for self-mutilation; to ensure that the system of organ allocation is as equitable as possible; and to enshrine in society the principle of "gifting."

The greatest shortcoming of this system is that it does not result, at least at present, in a sufficient number of cadaveric organs for all who would benefit from them. Whether any system (or any ethically defensible system) could entirely solve the organ "shortage" is an open question. But there are reasons to believe that new monetary incentives or more aggressive organ retrieval would increase the organ supply.

Public Recognition and Community Pressure ("Honoring and Shaming"):

One proposal for increasing the organ supply is to publicly honor—with medals or ceremonies, not compensation—those individuals (or their surviving families) who donate their organs. This proposal rests on the belief that donation to save life is a (*prima facie* [on the face of it]) civic duty, not just a philanthropic option. Often combined with this proposed policy of honoring organ donors is a proposal for civic "shaming" of those who are not organ donors—with slogans like "Friends don't let their friends waste the gift of life" or the creation of public registries so that community members can exhort their fellow non-donating citizens.

The likelihood that such a program would increase organ supply is of course uncertain. The only objection one can imagine to public recognition of organ donors is that recognition might become (at least partly) the reason for donating, and thus the donation might become less an "other-regarding" gift and more a "self-regarding" act. The idea of civic "shaming" of non-organ donors raises more questions: for example, whether individuals or families might have morally legitimate or morally admirable reasons (such as religious belief) for *not* donating their organs. It forces us to reflect on the difference between "asking" for organs and "expecting" them, and the difference between "charity" and "obligation."

Public Compensation ("Paying and Providing"):

In recent years, there have been a number of different proposals for compensating individuals or their surviving families for allowing their organs to be used (notice: it becomes less accurate, perhaps inaccurate, to call it "donation" once payment is involved). The primary goal of these proposals is to increase organ supply by motivating more individuals and families (with cash payment or other "valuable consideration") to allow their organs to be retrieved. In addition, such a policy could offer public recognition and honor to those who benefit society by allowing their organs to be retrieved. These proposals take different forms: some offer full or partial reimbursement of funeral expenses; some offer tax credits or rebates; some offer direct cash payment. Defenders of such compensation proposals often seek to distinguish them from organ markets: the compensation would be public, not private, and thus would represent the appreciation of the entire community rather than a private contract between parties; a compensation system would set firm limits on what could be compensated—for example, allowing reimbursement for funerals of the deceased but not payment for living donors who wish to sell one of their organs; and a compensation system for procurement would be kept separate from the system of organ allocation so as not to endanger the equity of organ allocation, whereas the right to sell one's organs in the open market might also mean giving special advantages to wealthy prospective recipients.

It is impossible to know in advance what effect such a policy would have on increasing organ supply; this depends both on the reasons why many individuals and families do not currently [as of 2003] allow their organs to be retrieved and on the size of the compensation, if in fact individuals or families have a price above which the "costs" of giving up their organs are outweighed by the monetary benefits. The greatest objection to such a policy is that it opens the door to a greatly increased commodification of the body; that it puts different prices on different body parts; that it risks creating new tensions and new divisions between surviving family members at the bedside about whether or not to take the money; and that it changes the character of organ procurement from "giving" to "selling," and thus undermines the civic purpose of teaching "charity."

Organ Markets ("Selling and Buying"):

There have been a number of proposals in recent years for organ markets, which would allow individuals before death or surviving family members after death to sell their own or their loved one's organs in private contracts. The primary goal of this system is to increase organ supply while respecting and expanding autonomy over one's body or the bodies of one's loved ones. Such market proposals take many different forms. These include "Futures Markets," where individuals agree before death to sell their organs and receive cash payment or lowered health-insurance rates while still living; and "Spot Markets," where families decide after death to sell their loved one's organs for cash payment or some other valuable consideration. Some proposals would have a market system for procurement only—thus allowing private selling but restricting private buying; other proposals would have both private buying and selling. Advocates for such policies argue that organ markets would be more efficient than public compensation, by allowing the price for different body parts to shift with shifting supply and demand. They also argue that it is unfair for everyone in the transplantation business to be making money except for the person who provides the precious organs.

As with public compensation, it is impossible to know in advance what effect any of these organ market policies, if enacted, would have on increasing the organ supply. Many of the same objections that are made to a public compensation system (see above) are made against organ markets—with the added argument that markets entail the full-scale (not partial) transformation of the body into property; and that organ markets promise to make organ allocation more unequal, since the benefits of a market system ultimately will require the freedom to buy at any price as well as freedom to sell at any price. Moreover, a market system risks creating conflicts between insurance companies, who "own" the rights to the organs of the deceased individuals who sold them, and the surviving family.

Routine Retrieval ("Taking and Getting"):

A final policy option is so-called "routine retrieval" or "presumed consent," in which it becomes standard policy to retrieve all usable organs after death, unless individuals or surviving families expressly request that such organs not be retrieved. The primary aim of such a policy is to increase organ supply, while at the same time eliminating the difficult task of requesting organs from family members moments after a loved one has died and the need for a public campaign encouraging people to become organ donors. There are different versions of this policy—ranging from those that make non-retrieval of organs relatively easy to those that make it relatively difficult. A version of this policy has been attempted in many European countries with mixed results.

While such a system seems likely to increase the supply of organs, it does so at a cost: staking a claim to the deceased and his or her body without individual or family consent. At the same time, it would change the character of organ procurement from "giving" to "taking," and thus undermine the civic purpose of teaching charity or the opportunity for individuals to be charitable. It would greatly expand the power of the state, forcing families to claim "possession" of the deceased body only so that they might proceed with rites of "surrender and separation."

There Is No Perfect Solution

The debate over organ transplantation touches on many of the deepest issues in bioethics: the obligation of healing the sick and its limits; the blessing and the burden of medical progress; the dignity and integrity of bodily life; the dangers of turning the body, dead or alive, into just another commodity; the importance of individual consent and the limits of human autonomy; and the difficult ethical and prudential judgments required when making public policy in areas that are both morally complex and deeply important. It is no exaggeration to say that our attitudes about organ transplantation say much about the kind of society that we are, both for better and for worse.

In the end, we are forced to accept the "tragic" nature of each of the above policy proposals—to accept that some goods are inevitably given up in order to preserve other goods that are deemed to be more important. And yet, by setting moral limits and outlawing "cash for flesh," we may be decreasing organ supply—and thus accepting the suffering and death of those we might have saved, at least temporarily. By setting aside those moral limits—by treating the body as property—in the hope of increasing organ supply, we risk devaluing the very human life (and human bodies) that we seek to save. It is of course possible that current opposition to organ markets or public compensation will someday seem as quaint and misguided as opposition to organ transplantation itself. No doubt the taboos of the past—such as respect for dead bodies—have stood in the way of much that is good about modern life and modern medicine. But it is also possible that the sweeping aside of some old taboos has lessened us, dehumanized us, and corrupted us. It is this risk of corruption and dehuman-ization that we must not fail to recognize, even as we seek to ameliorate suffering and cure disease by every ethical means possible. The specific question before us is this: What is the most ethically responsible and prudent public policy for pro-curing cadaver organs? Should the current law be changed, modified, or preserved?

2

Being a Kidney Donor Was a Good Choice for Me

Virginia Postrel

Virginia Postrel is a freelance writer and columnist for many publications, including the Atlantic, New York Times *business section, and* Forbes.

More than 66,000 Americans are on the waiting list for approximately 6,700 kidneys that become available each year as a result of someone's death. Cadavers are not the only source of kidneys, though. It is possible for healthy individuals to donate a kidney without sacrificing their own health. Becoming a kidney donor requires surgery, hospitalization, and recovery time. However, it does provide a very satisfying way of helping another person.

Until last November, I'd never thought about being a kidney donor. I hadn't known anyone with kidney disease, and like most people, I hadn't filled out an organ donation form when I'd gotten my driver's license. I'd never even donated blood. That all changed after I ran into a friend and asked, "How's Sally?" I got an unexpected answer: "She's . . . all right," in a tone that made it clear she was most definitely not all right.

Sally Satel and I have been friends since 1997. We're kindred spirits—strong-willed, intellectual iconoclasts who are a bit too ingenious for our own good. But she lives in Washington, D.C., where she's a fellow at a think tank, and I live in

Dallas. We almost never see each other and communicate mostly by e-mail. We follow each other's work but don't share our day-to-day lives. Last fall, no one would have called us close. So I had no idea Sally's kidneys were failing. She needed a transplant, our friend told me. Otherwise, she'd soon be on dialysis, tied at least three days a week to a machine that would filter poisons from her blood. For someone who prizes her independence and freedom of movement as much as Sally does, dialysis would have been a prison sentence.

With no spouse, children, siblings, or parents to offer her a kidney, I thought she must be desperate. I knew the chances of getting a cadaver kidney were low, although I didn't realize how truly miniscule: More than 66,000 Americans are on the waiting list for the 6,700 or so cadaver kidneys that are available each year. Just thinking about her situation made my heart race with empathetic panic.

Coming Up with a Plan

"Maybe we can do something to get Sally a kidney," I said. It probably sounded as if I were proposing a publicity campaign. After all, she and I and our mutual friend are in the persuasion business: We write books and articles and have lots of press connections. What I really meant, though, was "Maybe I can give Sally a kidney." At the time, it seemed like a perfectly natural reaction.

Usually when someone is seriously ill, all you can do is lend moral support and maybe cook some meals or run a few errands. Nothing you do will make that person well. But if you donate a kidney, you can (with the help of a team of medical specialists) cure her. Who wouldn't want to do it? I had no idea what a strange thought that was.

Nor did I sort through my motivations. I've spent a good bit of my life trying to save the world, mostly by working to beat back bad government policies, including some that would have stifled medical research. But even when your side wins, the victory is incremental and rarely permanent. And people of goodwill dedicated to the same good cause can be awfully contentious about how to achieve their goals.

All a donor and a recipient have to have in common is a compatible blood type; anti-rejection drugs take care of the rest.

In this case, there was something reassuring about the idea that the benefit wouldn't depend at all on my talents, persuasiveness, or intellect. It would be simple. All I had to do was show up. In middle age, I've realized that I can't save the world. But maybe I could save Sally. Someone had to.

Researching the Issue

Except for living in Texas, I was the ideal candidate. I was healthy, with no family history of kidney disease. Like Sally, I had no kids depending on me. (Unlike her, I had a big family of potential kidney donors, just in case.) I was self-employed, and my husband, a professor, had a fairly flexible schedule. Neither home nor work obligations would pose a problem.

But first I had research to do. I didn't want anyone to know I was considering the idea unless I was absolutely sure I'd go through with it. I didn't want to get Sally's hopes up and then renege. That would have been worse than not volunteering in the first place.

An hour on the Internet told me what I needed to know. All a donor and a recipient have to have in common is a compatible blood type; anti-rejection drugs take care of the rest. For the donor, the operation isn't especially risky or particularly difficult to recover from. Laparoscopic techniques have replaced the old side-splitting gashes with a few tiny holes and an incision two- to three-inches long, just big enough to slide out the kidney. The donor usually spends a couple of days in the hospital and, other than athletic exertions I'd shun anyway, can resume normal activities within a week or two. The main dangers are those of any major surgery: general anesthesia, bleeding, infection. They're serious risks, but people go through equally tough operations every day for purely cosmetic reasons.

Contrary to what most people think, living with one kidney is basically the same as living with two. The remaining organ grows to take up the slack. Someone with a single organ is no more vulnerable to kidney failure than someone with a pair, because most kidney disease attacks both at once. The exceptions are injuries, of course, and cancer. I was willing to take my chances.

To me, giving Sally a kidney was a practical, straightforward solution to a serious problem.

What about my husband? As I'd expected, he wasn't thrilled with the idea of letting someone slice open his wife, and he was afraid of the tiny but real risk that I might die. He liked Sally but didn't know her that well. He's a rational guy, however, and he knows what sort of person he married. He said okay.

Testing for Compatibility

I sent Sally a quick e-mail, confirming that she did in fact need a transplant. She already had a likely prospect, she said. "If your lead doesn't come through, let me know," I wrote back. "If I'm compatible, I'll be a donor." After a couple more exchanges, Sally put me in touch with her transplant coordinator.

The first step to becoming a kidney donor, I discovered, is to give blood—the easiest way to find out your blood type and, conveniently, a great test of squeamishness. My mother had always assured me that I was type O, like her, and thus a universal donor. Yet I didn't even make it to the blood typing.

Like many women, I was a shade anemic, with hemoglobin of 12.3 grams per deciliter instead of the required 12.5.

I went into training, eating iron-rich Total cereal for lunch every day. A week later, I hit the magic number, contributed a pint to the Texas blood supply, and a couple days after that, found out my blood type. Bad news: I was A positive, not universally compatible after all. "Will that work?" I e-mailed Sally. Miraculously, it would. She was also type A, but she didn't expect to need me.

I was to be the backup to "Bob from Canada," a guy Sally had found via matchhingdonors.com, a site for people looking for organ donors. The mysteriously generous Bob was our hero. (My husband was particularly fond of him.) But in mid-December, Sally suddenly lost touch with him. "I feel like Charlie Brown trying to kick the freaking football and Lucy keeps yanking it away," Sally e-mailed, asking me to get some basic blood and urine tests done in Dallas. By early January Bob was gone. A busy life had interfered with his good intentions.

Passing through Screening

Soon I was at the Washington Hospital Center, in D.C., filling lots of blood vials to make sure I had no diseases my kidney might pass along. I got an x-ray and an electrocardiogram. On a later trip, I met with a social worker, a nephrologist, and the surgeon, and I had a CT scan to confirm that I really had two healthy kidneys and determine which was the better of the two to take (in my case, the right).

The screening process was peculiarly gratifying. My brothers climb mountains and run marathons, and my parents work out with personal trainers three times a week, which makes me the family couch potato. My primary form of exercise is walking to restaurants. But compared with most would-be kidney donors—the not-so-healthy relatives of very sick people—I was a paragon of fitness: blood pressure on the low end of normal, no hepatitis C, no diabetes, an abdomen that these days passes for slim. (Laparoscopic surgery is more difficult, and sometimes impossible, if the donor is obese.) Everyone at the hospital was impressed. Yea for me!

Most important, it turned out, I had the right personality. Donating a kidney isn't, in fact, a matter of just showing up. You have to be pushy. Unless you're absolutely determined, you'll give up, and nobody will blame you—except, of course, the person who needs a kidney. When I went to see my Dallas doctor for preliminary tests, the first thing she said was "You know, you can change your mind."

Preparing for Surgery

To me, giving Sally a kidney was a practical, straightforward solution to a serious problem. It was important to her but not really a big deal to me. Until the surgery was scheduled—for Saturday, March 4—and I started telling people about it, I had no idea just how weird I was.

Normal people, I found, have a visceral—pun definitely intended—reaction to the idea of donating an organ. They're revolted. They identify entirely with the donor but not at all with the recipient. They don't compare kidney donation to other risky behavior, like flying a plane or running 31 miles to the bottom of the Grand Canyon and back, as my brother did last summer.

I was scared, of course—but of the surgery, not the loss of my kidney. I'd never been hospitalized before and, except for oral surgery when I was seven, had never had general anesthesia. Surgery, no matter how routine, is dangerous. The kidney is fed by a large renal artery and drained by a large renal vein. If the surgeon cut the wrong one, he'd have five seconds before I bled to death. (I didn't share this tidbit with my husband until after the operation.)

I did my taxes early so my husband wouldn't be stuck sorting through my business receipts if I were incapacitated, or worse. I arranged to stay at a friend's Washington crash pad. I asked the transplant coordinator to tell me, step-by-step, exactly what would happen once I got to the hospital so there would be no surprises.

Donating My Kidney

Things went pretty much as advertised. One minute Sally and I were on beds being wheeled down the hall. I was nervous for about two seconds.

And then I woke up. My husband and parents were there, looking relieved. The nurse took off my oxygen mask so they could feed me ice chips—not too many or I'd throw up. Eventually I moved on to water and clear foods, including tea to fight caffeine withdrawal. Sally had arranged a huge hotel-style room for me, complete with a sofa bed for my husband and real meals. He ate steak while I sipped broth and slurped lime Jell-O.

Yes, I did throw up. Three times and quite violently—a reaction to the anesthesia. I got used to answering a list of excretory questions, starting with "Have you passed gas?" After 24 hours on a catheter, my body refused for a while to urinate on command. When I learned to pee again, the nurse did a victory dance. All in all, it was a very dignified experience.

The worst moment was an early-morning visit by a grave, haggard surgeon—not mine but Sally's. What if Sally had died? What if giving her a kidney had killed her? I'd never seriously considered that possibility.

To my great relief, the surgeon said my friend was okay. But she had had a close call. She'd started hemorrhaging. They'd had to take her back into surgery to stop the bleeding. He'd done hundreds of these operations, and this had never happened. Sally was in intensive care. It had been a very long night.

A day later, when I was off my IV and able to walk through the hospital, we visited Sally. A tiny woman, she looked like a baby bird, with her short hair shooting up randomly and her skin slightly gray. She was groggy, a bit grouchy, and not entirely coherent. But she knew one thing clearly: "I almost died," she said.

On Tuesday we visited her again before leaving the hospital. She was still in the ICU but about to be moved. She looked like herself. She was talking to friends on her cell phone. What a relief.

The Road to Recovery

Sally left the hospital the following Sunday, the day I had my surgical staples removed. We joined her and a couple of friends for a messy hamburger lunch at her apartment. The next day, we flew home to Dallas.

I never had much pain and, once I left the hospital, took nothing stronger than aspirin, which my surgeon prescribed to prevent blood clots. But it took me about three weeks— longer than I expected—to get back to normal. The surgery had left me easily exhausted. Always a sleepy person, I was taking four-hour naps and falling behind on my deadlines.

Then suddenly I was myself again, with only an occasional twinge in what my husband calls the KV (for "kidney void") to remind me of my medical adventure. I caught up with my work and started traveling—short trips, with light luggage. My all-purpose excuse, "I just donated a kidney," had expired.

On April 10, less than six weeks after the surgery, Sally too went back to work. "I am waiting to be exhausted but I am not . . . darn," she wrote. "I may be back to normal. Don't think I am nuts but I liked being home and having everyone make a fuss."

She was finally better than before the operation. Her new kidney was working perfectly, she was no longer anemic, and she no longer had to take five medicines to ward off hypertension. I had never thought much of my kidney when I had it, but now it makes me proud.

She signed the e-mail "Spoiled in D.C."

3

Compensating the Families of Organ Donors Would Be Effective and Ethical

David E. Harrington and Edward A. Sayre

David E. Harrington is the Himmelright Professor of Economics at Kenyon College in Ohio. Edward A. Sayre is assistant professor of economics at Agnes Scott College in Georgia.

The policy of providing compensation to families has been effective in securing donations of cadavers that are used by medical schools for the training of doctors. A similar policy that reimbursed families of organ donors for funeral expenses could substantially increase the supply of organs available for transplantation.

Medical schools in the United States are awash in cadavers. Yet, at the same time, there is a chronic shortage of organs for transplant patients, resulting in the deaths of thousands of people each year. Understanding why so many people donate bodies to medical schools holds lessons for how we should reform the laws governing organ donations.

Alternatives to the Current System

Currently [as of 2006], U.S. medicine tries to procure transplant organs by urging people to register as organ donors. A recent report by the Institute of Medicine (IOM) on the se-

David E. Harrington and Edward A. Sayre, "Buying Bodies, Stealing Organs?" *Special to washingtonpost.com's Think Tank Town*, November 27, 2006. Copyright © 2006 Washingtonpost Newsweek Interactive. Reproduced by permission of the authors.

vere shortage of transplant organs proposes more of the same medicine but at a higher dose: In essence, it counsels that we should ask more fervently. But continuing this policy, no matter how fervently we solicit would-be donors, will only fail to prevent more unnecessary deaths and more reports on the chronic organ shortage.

An alternative proposal, currently under consideration in Canada, the UK and by the U.S. Department of Health and Human Services, is to legally entitle medical officials to "presume consent"—have authority to harvest organs from the recently deceased unless there is clear evidence that the donor would have objected. But some potential donors would have objected if asked prior to death, making this policy akin to stealing in some cases.

There is another effective way to increase the supply of transplant organs without the indignity and questionable ethics of presumed consent: offer would-be donors and their families some sort of compensation for agreeing to post-mortem donations.

Many public intellectuals, including the members of the IOM's organ donation panel, have raised all sorts of objections to this idea, and they argue that no compensation should be allowed unless there is clear empirical evidence that it would increase the supply of transplant organs. At the same time, compensation opponents decry the idea of creating a pilot program to obtain the empirical information they require. Despite those constraints, we have found clear empirical evidence that even modest compensation can dramatically affect donation decisions.

Medical schools routinely pay for the cremation or burial (often with elaborate memorial ceremonies) of the people whose bodies were donated to them for medical research and student training. In contrast, it is against federal law to offer any compensation for transplant organ procurement, including paying for organ donors' funeral expenses. This creates a bizarre asymmetry in the treatments of organ and whole body donations.

The Case for Compensation

Given the current cost of funerals, the savings from donating bodies to medical schools can be substantial. This is especially true in states with funeral industry-protective regulations that are intended to keep out low-cost competitors. Those states provide us an opportunity to test empirically the effects of compensation on whole-body donation and, in turn, to extrapolate whether there is any merit to the criticisms of organ donation compensation.

Surely if funeral service payments increase the donation rate of whole bodies, similar compensation would increase the donation rate of transplant organs.

If potential whole body donors respond to financial incentives, then we ought to see more body donations in stringently regulated states where funeral prices are higher. That is, in fact, what the data show. The number of body donations in stringently regulated states is 7.6 bodies per thousand deaths and only 3.2 bodies per thousand in unregulated states. This is powerful evidence that people react to financial incentives in making whole body donation decisions. We estimate that high funeral prices in the 38 states with stringent funeral regulations increase the number of donations by 8,400 bodies per year. It stands to reason that financial incentives would also raise the donation of transplant organs.

The IOM's rejection of such proposals rests on the argument that offering modest compensation would be perceived by organ donors as sullying their gift. But the empirical data on whole-body donation discredit the IOM's argument; the families of whole-body donors often proudly highlight their gifts in obituaries, despite their receiving the financial benefit of not having to pay for a funeral.

The empirical data also discredit the IOM's argument that financial incentives would not increase the supply of transplantable organs. Surely if funeral service payments increase the donation rate of whole bodies, similar compensation would increase the donation rate of transplant organs.

It is time the IOM and other public intellectuals accept the empirical data and set aside their dubious arguments against donor compensation. To continue the status quo or to adopt a presumed consent policy are both morally unacceptable. Allowing donor compensation would protect the dignity of donors and would reduce the suffering and death of the many people waiting for transplant organs.

4

People Who Need Transplants Should Be Allowed to Purchase Organs

Sally Satel

Sally Satel, MD, is a resident scholar at the American Enterprise Institute.

It is against the law in the United States for money, or anything of value, to be exchanged for a human organ. As a result, the demand for organs that can be used for transplants far exceeds the available supply. A free market for organs would provide economic incentives for organ donation and help assure that the supply of organs more adequately meets the needs of chronically ill persons who can be helped by a transplant.

A year ago [2005], I was searching the Internet for something rare and valuable: a human kidney. In August 2004, I learned I had end-stage renal disease and would need a transplant. At the time, my prospects for a donation from family or friends looked bleak, and I would soon have to begin dialysis. I would be hooked up to a machine three days a week for four hours at a time. This would continue for at least five years—the time it would take for a kidney from a deceased donor to become available. Even with dialysis, the kidneys of many sick people deteriorate so quickly that time runs out. An average of eleven Americans die each day waiting for a renal transplant.

Sally Satel, M.D., "Organs for Sale," *American Enterprise Institute for Public Policy*, November 21, 2006. Copyright © 2006 American Enterprise Institute for Public Policy Research. Reproduced with permission of The American Enterprise, a national magazine of Politics, Business, and Culture (TAEmag.com).

Searching for a Donor

Waiting for a kidney from a deceased donor is such a risky business that some people try publicly to convince strangers to give them live organs. Some put up billboards ("I NEED A KIDNEY, CAN YOU HELP? Call. . ."), start websites (GordyNeedsAKidney.org, whose opening page carries the plaintive headline, "Please Help Our Dad"), or go overseas to become "transplant tourists" on the Chinese black market with the frightful knowledge that the organ they get will almost surely come from an executed political prisoner. The desperation, as I found myself, is perfectly understandable. I have no siblings. Several friends said they would look into it—donors don't need to be genetically related—but they turned out to have disqualifying medical problems or spouses who objected, or they grew scared.

> *Only about one-third of Americans have designated themselves as donors on their driver's licenses or on state-run donor registries.*

Last fall, I turned to a website called MatchingDonors .com—which "matches" mostly prospective kidney donors with recipients—and quickly found a prospective donor. But six weeks later, he changed his mind. Then my wonderful friend Virginia Postrel came along. We are both healthy after a transplant operation on March 4 [2006] at the Washington Hospital Center. If Virginia had not donated her kidney, I could have languished on dialysis for years. Indeed, when I joined the national queue in January 2005, there were about 60,000 other people ahead of me, according to the nonprofit United Network for Organ Sharing (UNOS), which maintains the list under a monopoly contract with the federal government.

The Waiting List Is Growing

Today [November 2006], there are 67,600 people waiting for a posthumous kidney. In big cities, where the ratio of needy patients to available organs is highest, the wait—spent on dialysis, a procedure that circulates your blood through a machine that purifies it and returns it to your body—is up to eight years. Last year, only 16,470 people received kidneys; roughly half of the donors were deceased, and half were living. Meanwhile, 4,100 died waiting. By 2010, the wait will be at least ten years, exceeding the average length of time that adults on dialysis survive.

More and more physicians, ethicists, economists, and legal scholars are urging the legalization of payments for organs in order to generate more kidneys for transplantation.

Despite decades of public education about the virtues of donating organs at death, the level of such gifts has remained disappointingly steady. Only about one-third of Americans have designated themselves as donors on their driver's licenses or on state-run donor registries. For the rest, the decision to donate organs will fall to family members, who about half the time deny the requests of hospitals. More important, however, is that very few of the Americans who die, perhaps 13,000 a year (or less than 1 percent of all deaths), possess organs healthy enough for transplanting—so even if every family consented, the need for thousands of kidneys would go unmet.

The chasm between the number of available kidneys and the number of people needing one will widen each year. This is due to our misplaced faith in the power of altruism. The "transplant community," as it is called—organizations that encourage funding and gifts of organs, and many surgeons and nephrologists—expects people, both living donors and loved ones of the deceased, to give a body part and to receive nothing in return. In fact, it is illegal in the United States to receive money or anything of value ("valuable consideration") in exchange for an organ, a principle set down by Congress in 1984 in the National Organ Transplantation Act.

Compensation Is Needed

Don't get me wrong. Altruism is a beautiful thing—it's the reason I have a new kidney—but altruism alone cannot resolve the organ shortage. For that reason, more and more physicians, ethicists, economists, and legal scholars are urging the legalization of payments for organs in order to generate more kidneys for transplantation. One doesn't need to be Milton Friedman [a Nobel Prize-winning economist] to know that a price of zero for anything virtually guarantees its shortage.

Any medical center or physician who objects to the practice of compensating donors can simply opt out of performing transplants that use such organs.

"Is it wrong for an individual. . .who wishes to utilize part of his body for the benefit of another [to] be provided with financial compensation that could obliterate a life of destitution for the individual and his family?" asked Dr. Richard Fine, president of the American Society of Transplantation, in his address to the World Transplant Congress this year.

Supporters of experimenting with a market for organs encounter an array of objections, theoretical and practical. One popular argument, first advanced by Richard M. Titmuss, professor of social administration at the London School of Economics, is that altruism is the sole legitimate impulse behind organ donation. In 1971, Titmuss, a dedicated socialist and member of the Fabian Society, published *The Gift Relationship: From Human Blood to Social Policy*, which rapidly became a U.S. bestseller. He argued that altruistic acts are among the most sensitive indicators of the quality of human relationships and values in a society. Capitalism, on the other hand, is morally bankrupt.

This ethic is very much alive among the bureaucrats that run the United Network for Organ Sharing, which manages the transplant list. "Organ transplantation is built upon altruism and public trust. If anything shakes that trust, then everyone loses," says the UNOS website. Yet the trust is already badly rattled. "The current system has degenerated into an equal opportunity to die on the waiting list," observes nephrologist [kidney treatment specialist] Benjamin Hippen, who advocated compensating donors (or perhaps they should be called "vendors") before the President's Council on Bioethics this summer.

Other Objections

Another theoretical objection to compensating donors is the notion that it will "commodify" the body and thus dehumanize the rest of us, let alone the person who gives his kidney in exchange for "valuable consideration." Yet with proper respect for donors and informed consent, it strikes me that careful engagement in financial arrangements is far less distasteful than allowing people to suffer and die. These are not abstract people, mind you, like the ones who may well be helped by stem cell discoveries years down the road, but live humans like the 49-year-old former secretary from the Pentagon I met last summer. For four years now, every Monday, Wednesday, and Friday, she has been sitting in Chair No. 7 in the dialysis center a few blocks from our offices.

Others go so far as to reject the very premise that saving lives is a paramount goal of medicine. "If we turn organ procurement into a crusade, we make of death simply a problem to be solved rather than an event to be endured as best we can, with whatever resources of mind and spirit are available to us," says Gilbert Meilaender, professor of theological ethics at Valparaiso University and a member of the President's Council on Bioethics. Now, it is one thing to question whether we should prolong the life of a vegetative patient, but quite another to abandon treatments for renal failure under circumstances in which a well-established remedy (transplantation) already exists—a remedy whose economic cost to society is lower than the cost of the less effective alternative, dialysis.

The Risks Are Small

This is a good time to point out that the live donor—or vendor—of a kidney is exposed to only minor risks, the most significant being those associated with anesthesia and surgery itself—0.03% mortality—comparable to any other operation. Because the surgery is done using a laparoscopic approach, the visible scar is only 2 fo 3 inches long. My donor, Virginia, was out of the hospital in three days and back to writing her magazine column a week later.

Long-term risks are also low. Typical is a 1997 study from Norway that followed 1,332 kidney donors for an average of 32 years. It found no difference in mortality rates between people who give kidneys and the general population. A 25-year follow-up of seventy donors conducted by the Cleveland Clinic found that the renal function is "well preserved" and that the overall incidence of hypertension was comparable to that of non-donors. The truth is that a normal person can get along perfectly well with one kidney. The risk a donor runs is that his single functioning kidney will become diseased or injured, and he'll need a transplant himself—a highly unlikely event.

Perhaps the most vocal critic of compensating donors is the National Kidney Foundation. It is offended by the idea that a donor might benefit in ways other than the psychic reward of pure giving. States NKF chairman Charles Fruit: "Families decide to donate the organs of a loved one for altruistic reasons. Payment is an affront to those who have already donated." Virginia, a take-no-prisoners journalist, responded pointedly to Fruit on her website, www.dynamist.com. "The argument that paying organ donors is 'an affront' to unpaid donors is disgusting. Are unpaid donors giving organs to save lives or just to make themselves feel morally superior? Even in the latter case, they shouldn't care if other people get paid."

Finding Middle Ground

In the end, moral objections such as these put us at a stand-off. I doubt I could change the mind of Professor Meilaender, who sincerely believes that organ donation violates what it means to be human. And there's nothing he can say to dissuade me from believing that free, informed, and willing individuals should be able to participate in a regulated exchange involving valuable consideration. Thus, the meaningful question becomes how both sides can honor their moral commitments.

The best answer is by creating a market arrangement to exist in parallel with altruistic giving. Within such a framework, any medical center or physician who objects to the practice of compensating donors can simply opt out of performing transplants that use such organs. Recipients on the list are free to turn down a paid-for organ and wait for one given altruistically. Choice for all—donors, recipients, and physicians—is enhanced. And it is choice in the greater service of diminishing sickness and death. Paradoxically, the current system based on altruism-or-else undermines the individual autonomy that is at the heart of the most widely held values in bioethics.

Not all objections to donor compensation, however, are abstract. A common concern is the potential for exploiting donors—especially low-income donors, who, as the critics reasonably claim, will be the most likely to find incentives attractive. Without question, protecting donors is enormously important. That is why any plan for compensation should be regulated. Potential donors must receive education about what it means to donate a kidney and the risks they run. They must undergo careful medical and psychological screening and receive quality follow-up care.

Critics often point to the horror stories from transplant black markets overseas and hold them up as cautionary tales. But the catastrophists have it exactly backward. It is when payment is not an above-board part of the medical system that black markets lead to minimal education of prospective donors, poor post-operative and follow-up care, and failure to honor agreements for payment.

Finally, some critics argue we have no evidence that an incentive system would work. True. So we need experimentation. Frankly, I don't know what the perfect kidney market would look like, but let's assume that Congress makes a bold and common-sense move and amends current law to permit the exchange of money or something of value for a kidney. Here are several alternative market systems:

A Forward Market for Cadaver Organs

Economist Lloyd Cohen proposed one of the first market-based models to increase the number of cadaver organs. Potential donors would either (1) be paid a small amount today by the government or insurance companies to join the current donor registry, or (2) register today in return for the possibility of a much larger payment to their estates should the organs be used at death.

The advantage of such a forward-looking approach is that the decision-making burden is taken off family members at a painful time—when they are sitting in the emergency room learning that someone they love is now brain-dead. And, of course, there is no worry of exploiting the donor. A forward market could also help satisfy the 23,000 people waiting for livers, hearts, and lungs.

But deceased donors cannot meet the need for kidneys. In addition, kidneys from live donors are healthier than those obtained after death and survive, typically, for 10 to 20 years (or one-third longer). Thus, to mitigate the shortage of kidneys, we must consider offering incentives to people amenable to relinquishing one while they are alive.

The Centralized Single Compensator Approach

In this approach, the federal government or a designated agency acts as the only authority with the power to buy and allocate organs for transplants. As is currently the case with cadaver organs, kidneys obtained through compensated donors would be matched with the next best candidate waiting on the national list.

Under this scheme, Medicare would underwrite the incentives in light of the fact that it already pays for dialysis treatment under the 1972 End Stage Renal Disease (ESRD) amendment to the Social Security Act. This entitlement provides care for Americans with terminal renal failure regardless of age if they have met required work credits for Social Security. Last year, the ESRD program spent about $16 billion on dialysis, or about $66,000 per patient annually. Since a 35-year-old spends about nine years on dialysis, the total cost is around $600,000; for a 64-year-old, about four years at $300,000. Compare these expenses with the cost of a transplant operation—approximately $75,000 in all for the one-time cost of the surgeries and hospital stays of the donor and recipient, plus the first year of follow-up medical care (including medicine).

In most cases, these savings would easily pay for a lifetime supply of the expensive immunosuppressant drugs to prevent rejection of the new kidney. The drugs cost $15,000 to $20,000 a year, and every recipient must take them every day for life. Medicare pays for transplant surgery but stops reimbursing for the drugs, at 80 percent of full price, three years post-transplant if the patient goes back to work.

Methods of Compensation

What kinds of compensation should be offered? A reasonable case could be made for an outright payment—after all, it is hard to argue that an individual is competent enough to sell an organ yet unfit to manage the money he receives in exchange for it—but I am partial to a compromise approach in order to defuse those who say that people will sell their organs for quick cash or use it to buy something frivolous. For example, the donor could choose from a menu of options, including a deposit to a 401(k) retirement plan, tax credits, tuition vouchers for the donor's children, long-term nursing care, family health coverage, life and nonfatal injury insurance, a charitable contribution in the donor's name, or cash payments stretched over time.

Donor protection is the lynchpin of any compensation model. Standard guidelines for physical and psychological screening, donor education, and informed consent could be formulated by a medical organization, such as the American Society of Transplant Surgeons, or another entity designated by the federal Department of Health and Human Services. A "waiting period" of three to six months could be built in to ensure the prospective donor has ample time to think it through. Monitoring donor health post-transplant is important as well. One idea is to provide lifetime health insurance, through Medicare or a private insurer for the donor. He would receive annual physicals, routine medical screening, and long-term follow-up in addition to standard health coverage. A federally sponsored registry of donors could help us study long-term outcomes for donors and vendors and take steps to remedy physical or psychological difficulties that arise.

Other Approaches

In this scheme, donors, compensators (that is, the entities that pay for the transplants), and medical centers (that perform them) would be coordinated with one another through an intermediary broker. Medicare would be one of several possible compensators, along with private insurers, charitable foundations, or a fund established perhaps through a surcharge added to the cost paid by insurers and foundations.

The easiest way to start a market for organs is simply to change the law to allow someone who needs an organ and someone who wants to sell one to make their own arrangements through contract—as infertile couples currently do with surrogate mothers. But such a system would inevitably attract criticism because it appears to favor well-off sick people over poor.

While private contracts may seem unfair because only those with means will be able to purchase directly, poor people who need kidneys would be no worse off—and, very likely, considerably better off—than under the current system. First, a stranger interested in selling a kidney is unlikely to give it away for free to the next person on the list (only 88 donors last year made such anonymous gifts); thus, few poor people would be deprived of kidneys they would otherwise have gotten voluntarily. Second, anyone who gets a kidney by contract is removed from the waiting list, and everyone behind him benefits by moving up. Third, private charities could offer to help subsidize the cost for a needy patient or pay outright.

Under an enforceable but private contract, a compensated donor would be treated no differently from an altruistic one. There would still be federal or state regulation. The donor would undergo rigorous medical and psychological screening at an established transplant center, receive guidance on informed consent, and have both a waiting period and the opportunity to drop out of the process at any point. No transplant center would dream of risking its reputation or loss of

Medicare funding by not performing quality screening. (As for the converse argument—that, despite all the safeguards, poor people will be tempted by money to sell a kidney they really want to keep—why not simply bar anyone with an income under $35,000 a year from giving a kidney? Another version of this approach, suggested by Virginia's economist husband, would be to give a one-year tax holiday to donors. That way, the rich would have a far bigger incentive to donate an organ than the poor.)

A Moral Imperative for Change

These broad proposals, and variants on them, need considerable elaboration. Many questions remain: How would prices be determined? Would each available kidney be allotted to the next well-matched person on the list? Or should living organs be preferentially allocated to the healthiest people on the list—that is, those who will get the most "life" out of the organ? Could noncitizens be paid donors? Also, could people have a say in who would receive their kidneys? As it currently stands, most living donors give altruistically because they are trying to help a friend or relative, not a stranger. But it is surely possible that the decision of an ambivalent friend could tip in the direction of giving with the promise of compensation. And since each patient on dialysis is functionally "attached" to a Medicare entitlement, perhaps the recipient could direct a portion of "his" Medicare allotment to his friend as payment.

There is no denying the political and practical challenges that come with introducing payment into a 20-year-old scheme built on the premise that generosity is the only legitimate motive for giving. Yet as death and suffering mount, constructing a market-based incentive program to increase the supply of transplantable organs has become a moral imperative. Its architects must give serious consideration to principled reservations and to concerns about donor safety, but repugnance and caution are not in themselves arguments against innovation. They are only reasons for vigilance and care.

5

The Sale of Organs Would Undermine Fundamental Values

Francis L. Delmonico, MD

Francis L. Delmonico, MD, is a transplant surgeon and a representative of the National Kidney Foundation (NKF).

Surveys show that significant numbers of live kidney donors experience burdensome expenses in connection with their organ donation. The National Kidney Foundation favors measures that would provide for remuneration of expenses in connection with the act of kidney donation. However, the exchange of body parts itself should not be allowed to become a financial transaction. A system that provided financial compensation for body parts would distort the doctor-patient relationship, diminish dignity, and devalue human life.

Good Morning. I am Francis Delmonico, a transplant surgeon at Massachusetts General Hospital, Professor of Surgery at Harvard Medical School, and a volunteer for the National Kidney Foundation (NKF), as a member of the NKF's Medical and Scientific Advisory Board. On behalf of the 30,000 members of the NKF, including several thousand solid organ transplant recipients, we appreciate the opportunity to present testimony today.

The NKF acknowledges the support that Congress has provided for organ donation in legislation to assist living or-

Francis L. Delmonico, "Testimony of the National Kidney Foundation, Subcommittee on Oversight and Investigation," *U.S. House of Representatives*, June 3, 2003. Reproduced by permission.

gan donors with non-medical expenses such as travel and subsistence, which is included in the recent House passage of H.R. 399, the "Organ Donation Improvement Act of 2003." Surveys of living kidney donors conducted by the NKF have revealed that 1 in 4 respondents experienced a burden with non-reimbursed expenses. We are encouraged that H.R. 399 will enhance the opportunity for live organ donation.

Any attempt to assign a monetary value to the human body or its body parts, even in the hope of increasing organ supply, diminishes human dignity and devalues the very human life we seek to save.

Payment for Organs Would Be Unethical and Corrupting

Remuneration or expenses related to donation, whether living or non-living, is ethically different than a monetary payment that enriches a person as the motivation to be an organ donor. The National Organ Transplant Act (NOTA) of 1984 prohibits anyone from acquiring, receiving, or transferring a human organ for valuable consideration for use in human transplantation. The NKF supports this legislation because the sale of bodies or body parts would undermine the fundamental values of our society. Payments would exploit the most vulnerable members of our society, with the degree of exploitation influenced by gender, ethnicity, and the social status of the vendor. This exploitation has been the experience of a black market for organs throughout the world. To suggest that the Federal Government or individual States be the proprietor of a market for organs is contrary to the proper role of government. For those global economists who would import a poor person into this country even for the noble reason to feed her family by selling her kidney, the NKF would ask: will these market forces next suggest that our government sanction her selling a part of her liver, then a lobe of her lung?

Advocacy for organ vendors (versus donors) also presents an inherent conflict for the physician's professional relationship with a patient. In that relationship, patients are not clients or commodities. It should be evident that money as a motivation for "donation" distorts the basis of the physician-patient relationship: the trust of each other. The medical decision and procedure that may be forced upon the organ seller and the physician are not by the priority of best care, but rather by the dictate of the sale.

Organ sellers are now reported to know the difference between a proper patient-physician relationship and the complicated interaction they have experienced, much to their regret. These unfortunate individuals are not considered as patients but objects of an arbitrary monetary calculation, driven by the going rate in the market place (government regulated or not). Any attempt to assign a monetary value to the human body or its body parts, even in the hope of increasing organ supply, diminishes human dignity and devaluates the very human life we seek to save.

Proponents of financial incentives for non-living organ donation assert that demonstration projects should be conducted to determine whether it will increase the organ supply. However, the NKF believes that it is impossible to separate the ethical debate of financial incentives for non-living donation from the unethical practice of selling human organs. Payments for organs could undermine the integrity of the organ donor pool as was the experience of paid blood donations. Furthermore, the advocates of such demonstration projects have given no formula as to how they will make a distinction of endorsing live donor sales, nor have they assured appropriate ethical oversight to prevent potential donor families from perceiving this project as merely a payment for organs.

For demonstration projects of financial incentives to be initiated in the United States, it will require a revision of the federal law by Congress. The consequence of a congressional endorsement of a payment for organs would be profound. It could propel other countries to sanction an unethical and unjust standard of immense proportions, one in which the wealthy readily obtain organs from the poor, justified by the citation of congressional sanction. In that reality, the poor person will remain poor but lose health and maybe more than one organ in the process of a government authorized abuse of the poor for the rich.

Opposition to payment for organs is not limited to the NKF. The American College of Surgeons has said that compensation of any kind for organs is wrong. The president of the American Society of Transplant Surgeons (ASTS) has testified this morning that the ASTS opposes payments for living or deceased organs.

An Alternative Method

What can we all do now to increase deceased organ donation beyond recent efforts? The NKF commends the approach brought to the Committee's attention today by Robert Metzger of the United Network for Organ Sharing (UNOS) in concert with Joe Roth representing the Association of Organ Procurement Organizations (AOPO): to honor the potential organ donor's wishes. What better way could a mournful family reconcile some of its grief, than to honor their loved one's desire to provide an altruistic gift to individuals in need? The decedent's self-determination to donate should not be overruled. However, the NKF also wishes to underscore that while fulfilling donor wishes, the OPO and hospital staff must be sensitive to the needs of families at the time of crisis. The NKF supports the needs and expectations of donor families through its National Donor Family Council (NDFC), which we founded in 1992. With more than 10,000 donor family and professional members, the NDFC represents donors of all organs and tissues.

This approach of honoring the donor's wishes was the thrust behind the Uniform Anatomical Gift Act (UAGA) promulgated in every state many years ago and recently endorsed by the Secretary of Health's Advisory Committee on Transplantation. Thus, the NKF joins today with the all of the transplant community to create a timely national momentum to embrace a social responsibility conveyed by the donor authorization initiative. The NKF affirms the right of individuals to authorize the donation of their organs and tissues at death. This alternative approach to buying and selling organs brings an ethical consensus to which we all can devote ourselves.

6

The Organ Donation System Should Be Based on Quid Pro Quo

David J. Undis

David J. Undis is executive director of LifeSharers, an organization of people who have pledged that upon their death, their organs will be donated to fellow members when possible.

The present organ allocation system makes no distinction between those who have agreed to donate their organs and those who have not. This is unfair. The United Network for Organ Sharing, which operates the national organ allocation system, should make it a policy that organs will be made available for transplantation first to those individuals who are themselves registered organ donors. Only when there are no such individuals eligible to receive an organ should it be given to a non-organ donor. This change would greatly increase the incentive for individuals to become registered organ donors, with a resulting increase in the number of donated organs that would be adequate to overcome the present shortage of organs available for transplant.

In 2005, there were about 7,600 deceased organ donors in the United States. These generous people provided the organs for about 21,000 transplants. But organs are transplanted from less than half of the eligible deceased donors. That means Americans buried or cremated about 21,000 transplantable or-

David J. Undis, "Increasing Organ Donation Supply by Changing Organ Allocation," *Bio.com*, December, 2005. Reproduced by permission.

gans in 2005. To put that number in perspective, in 2005 about 6,300 people were removed from the national transplant waiting list because they died and 1,800 more were removed because they became too sick to undergo transplant surgery. We could eliminate most waiting list deaths, reduce the size of the waiting list, and shorten waiting times for people still on the list if we stopped throwing away so many transplantable organs.

Years and years of efforts to increase organ donation rates in the United States have largely failed. There were only about 2,000 more deceased organ donors in 2005 than there were in 1995. But there were over 50,000 more people waiting for transplants at the end of 2005 than there were at the end of 1995. Over 44,000 people joined the waiting list in 2005. There are over 95,000 people on the waiting list right now, and more than half of them will die before they get a transplant.

A Worsening Problem

The organ shortage continues to grow larger every year. Expanded use of "extended criteria" organs from deceased donors hasn't reduced the shortage. Neither has the large increase in the number of live donors. Improvements in procurement methods, the spread of state donor registries, and enactment of state laws making organ donation registrations legally binding haven't stopped the organ shortage from increasing either. The best that can be said about these efforts is that they've helped slow the increase in the shortage.

We should allocate organs first to people who have agreed to donate their own organs when they die.

Several other strategies for reducing the organ shortage have been suggested. These include the use of financial incentives, the enactment of presumed consent laws, and even "organ conscription" or mandatory donation. These strategies share a common weakness. None of them are currently legal. They all can be enacted only through legislative action, and they all face broad-based opposition making such action very unlikely.

Fortunately, there is an already-legal way to reduce the organ shortage. It has been largely overlooked but it would be extremely effective. We can increase the supply of organs by changing the organ allocation system.

A New Allocation System

We should allocate organs first to people who have agreed to donate their own organs when they die. This will create an incentive for more people to register as organ donors, and that incentive will save thousands of lives every year.

Imagine that the United Network for Organ Sharing, which operates the national organ allocation system, made the following announcement today: "Beginning January 1 of next year, we will make no human organ available for transplantation into any person who is not a registered organ donor. The only exceptions will be directed donations and cases where no registered organ donor matches an organ that is available."

Giving organs first to organ donors produces more organ donors, and that saves more lives.

Following the announcement of this policy change, millions and millions of people would register as organ donors. They would register their children as well. Anyone who registered as an organ donor would increase their chances of getting an organ if they ever needed one. Anyone who didn't register would reduce their chances. The decision to register could literally mean the difference between life and death. Agreeing to donate your organs after you die is a small price to pay for a better chance to get a transplant organ if you ever need one to live. Almost everyone would decide to pay that price. The supply of organs would increase significantly, and thousands of lives would be saved every year.

No medical breakthroughs are needed to save these lives. All we need is behavior change. All we need to do is convince people to stop throwing away organs that could save their neighbors' lives. Allocating organs first to registered organ donors would produce that behavior change.

A Proposal that Is Easy to Implement

No legislative action is needed to implement this change. UNOS already has the authority to give registered organ donors an allocation preference. The UNOS Ethics Committee acknowledged this fact in its 1993 white paper titled "Preferred Status For Organ Donors." They wrote: "a trial could be implemented without requiring any alteration in existing legislation."

In fact, UNOS already moves live donors up the waiting list if they later need a transplant. UNOS can, and should, do the same for people who agree to donate when they die.

It would be easy for UNOS to change its allocation system to put registered organ donors first. UNOS could add a single field to its waiting list database. That field would show whether or not a potential organ recipient is a registered organ donor. Then whenever an organ becomes available, instead of offering it first to the highest-ranked person on its match run, UNOS could offer it first to the highest-ranked registered donor.

Under UNOS' allocation rules, most organs are given to non-donors. UNOS allocates about 50% of all organs to people who haven't agreed to donate their own organs when they die. This highlights another reason to give organs first to registered organ donors—it makes the organ allocation system fairer.

It's just not fair to give organs to people who won't donate their own, when there are registered organ donors who need them. It's like awarding the lottery jackpot to someone who didn't buy a ticket.

A Matter of Justice

Giving organs first to registered organ donors is a simple matter of justice. Justice demands that people who are the same should be treated the same. But the person who hasn't agreed to donate his organs when he dies is not the same as the person who has. There is an ethically relevant difference between the two.

Imagine a liver is available for transplant. Imagine that two people are a good match for that liver—Mr. Donor, who has committed to donate his organs when he dies, and Mr. Keeper, who has not. Given that there is a shortage of organs, and given that Mr. Keeper's only alternatives to donating his organs are to bury them or cremate them, should we treat Mr. Donor and Mr. Keeper as if there is no ethically relevant difference between them? No, Mr. Keeper's failure to donate his organs is a spectacularly selfish act. He would throw away his organs instead of saving the lives of his neighbors— and those are his only available choices! It is mind-boggling to suggest that Mr. Keeper's claim to an organ has the same ethical basis as Mr. Donor's claim. Mr. Donor should get that liver, even if Mr. Keeper is sicker or has been waiting longer. Mr. Keeper has no moral claim to an organ. Giving the liver to Mr. Donor serves the cause of justice.

Perhaps more importantly, rewarding Mr. Donor's decision to donate his organs encourages others to do the same. That saves lives. On the other hand, giving that liver to Mr. Keeper encourages others to delay registering as organ donors or to refuse to register, and that lets more people on the transplant waiting list suffer and die.

Fairness Will Promote Generosity

Giving organs first to organ donors produces more organ donors, and that saves more lives. The primary goal of the organ allocation system should be to save as many lives as possible, and UNOS should change its allocation rules.

UNOS has the power to implement this simple change, but they have not yet chosen to do so. In 1993 the UNOS Ethics Committee recommended "wider societal discussion before considering concrete plans for implementation" of any system for giving preferred status to organ donors, but UNOS has not led that discussion. It has been largely silent on the subject. That is unfortunate. Over 60,000 people on the UNOS waiting list have died over the last 10 years. Most of those deaths could have been prevented.

Fortunately, as individuals we don't need to wait on UNOS to increase the organ supply from the top down. We can attack the problem from the ground up. We can allocate our own organs. We can offer them first to registered organ donors who will do the same for us. That is the premise behind LifeSharers.

LifeSharers

LifeSharers is a grass-roots organ donation network. Members agree to donate their organs when they die. Furthermore, they agree to offer their organs first to fellow members, if any member is a suitable match, before offering them to others. Membership is free and open to all at www.lifesharers.org. LifeSharers does not discriminate on the basis of race, color, religion, sex, sexual orientation, national origin, age, physical handicap, health status, marital status, or economic status. LifeSharers welcomes everyone, and turns no one away. Life-Sharers has over 8,000 members, including members in all 50 states and the District of Columbia. About 10% of LifeSharers members are minor children enrolled by their parents. Life-Sharers is organized as a 501(c)(3) nonprofit organization, it is staffed by unpaid volunteers, and its operations are funded by tax-deductible charitable contributions.

LifeSharers members offer their organs first to other registered organ donors using a form of directed donation that is legal under federal law and in all 50 states and the District of Columbia.

No LifeSharers member has yet [as of December 2005] died in circumstances that would have permitted recovery of their organs. At its current membership level, there is about a 33% chance that organs will be recovered from one or more LifeSharers members in the next twelve months. When members start getting organs from other members, LifeSharers expects a tremendous amount of publicity and a very large jump in membership.

But LifeSharers can't increase the organ supply as fast as UNOS could if it adopted the LifeSharers approach as its own. By allocating organs first to registered organ donors, UNOS could save thousands of lives every year. If UNOS acted today it would start saving those lives tomorrow.

7

Organ Donors Should be Reimbursed for Their Expenses

Scott Klarenbach, Amit X. Garg, and Sorina Vlaicu

Scott Klarenbach is an assistant professor in the Department of Medicine of the University of Alberta. He works in the Division of Nephrology and Transplantation Immunology.

While the economic benefits of living kidney donation for the recipient are well-known, the economic impact on the donor is not often considered. Donor costs include the expense of traveling to medical locations, tests, appointments, and hospital admissions, hotel accommodations, telephone bills, and incidental medical expenses following discharges. Also, donors often incur costs from time lost at work, impaired ability to work, and the need to hire help during the recovery period. Provisions should be made to allow compensation for the expenses incurred when individuals choose to become living organ donors.

Kidney transplantation from living donors is an established treatment for end-stage renal disease: it increases life expectancy, improves quality of life and is less costly than dialysis. In Canada, the growth of solid-organ transplantation over the past decade has primarily been attributable to increases in living organ donation, for which rates have doubled within the past decade. Nevertheless, waiting lists continue to grow, and further strategies to increase organ donations from living donors continue to be explored. Eliminating barriers to dona-

Scott Klarenbach, Amit X. Garg, and Sorina Vlaicu, "Living Organ Donors Face Financial Barriers: A National Reimbursement Policy Is Needed." Reprinted from *Canadian Medical Association Journal*, March 14, 2006, pp. 797–798. Copyright © 2006 CMA Media Inc. Reproduced by permission of the publisher.

tion is one way to increase donors. Currently [as of 2006] in this country, there are economic disincentives to donors that, in addition to being unfair, may limit rates of organ donation and need to be addressed with a national policy.

In one ... study, financial hardship or significant financial burden was reported by 23% of people who donated a kidney.

The economics of living kidney donation have been well described from the perspective of the recipient and health care payer: one living kidney donation is estimated to result in a net increase of 2 to 3.5 quality-adjusted life-years, and a net health care savings of $100,000. The economic impact to the donor, on the other hand, is infrequently considered, but is best understood by first considering all possible direct and indirect (productivity) costs incurred. Direct costs include all resources consumed from the perspective of the donor (which may not involve a direct monetary transaction), including travel for tests, appointments and hospital admission; accommodation; long-distance telephone charges; and incidental medical costs such as fees for medications after discharge. Indirect costs consist of the economic consequences of lost or impaired ability to work or engage in leisure activities, such as lost income and household costs related to domestic maintenance and chores as well as to dependent care.

Donation Has Significant Costs

The frequency and magnitude of these costs are not well described. The existing literature likely underestimates true costs and suffers from the retrospective nature of most reports of donor costs: lengthy time frames for patient recall, low response rates and incomplete capture of all the relevant costs. Nonetheless, it is clear that many donors are adversely affected by these costs. In one follow-up study, financial hardship or significant financial burden was reported by 23% of people who donated a kidney. In other examples, 53%–99% of donors experienced costs due to travel and accommodation in 2 North American studies, and 14%–30% lost income (averaging, in 2004 dollars, as much as $4,410).

Although the magnitude of these costs may not seem dramatic to some, the context in which they occur deserves consideration. Biological relatives and spouses make up the majority of living donors, who may already be burdened financially by the chronic medical illness of a family member. In a single-centre study involving 133 potential donors to a family member, 24% did not donate because of the anticipated financial hardship. This same study indicated that recipients with higher incomes were more likely to receive a kidney from a living donor, which suggests that household financial status may influence which recipients receive a living-donor, as opposed to a deceased-donor, kidney. A similar pattern of higher aggregate income level for those receiving a kidney from a living versus a deceased donor exists in Canada (unpublished data from the Canadian Organ Replacement Registry), and it is a reasonable assumption that economic consequences pose a larger burden to potential donors with a lower income. The existence of financial barriers to potential organ donors clearly runs contrary to our objective of increasing rates of organ donation in Canada.

Different Approaches to Reimbursement

Some countries, such as Hungary, Portugal, Slovakia and Turkey, do not permit any form of compensation for donors. This may stem from a desire to avoid a free or black market for organs. However, recent policies addressing reimbursement of the financial consequences incurred by donors have emerged internationally. The World Medical Association and the American Medical Association Council on Ethics and Judicial Affairs make a clear distinction between reimbursement of the expenses incurred through the donation process, which is expressly deemed permissible, and a market where payment for an organ results in financial gain.

Reimbursement is allowed implicitly in some countries, including Canada, whereas others have adopted explicit policies. In France, for example, transplant centres are required to reimburse donors for travel and accommodation expenses; and in the United Kingdom, the National Health Service is permitted, though not required, to reimburse lost wages as well as travel and accommodation costs.

We rely on altruistically motivated organ donors to improve the health of those with chronic disease.

Currently Canada does not have a national unified strategy to reimburse living organ donors. Before devising a strategy, it is important to identify existing services and infrastructure to deliver such a policy. Current federal initiatives include employment insurance and short-term disability as well as the tax credit for medical expenses. Provincial initiatives include coverage for medical services, limited travel coverage in some provinces (Newfoundland and Labrador, New Brunswick, Prince Edward Island and northern Ontario) and paid-leave programs (Saskatchewan). Assistance from nonprofit organizations such as the Kidney Foundation of Canada is potentialy available. However, the requirements necessary to receive employment insurance and benefits delivered through tax credits may work to the disadvantage of people who work in alternative arrangements or have a lower income, and all existing programs are limited in scope and availability.

A Program That Will Work

In a survey of key Canadian informants in the field of organ transplantation—sources working in transplant centres, provincial governments, professional associations, non-governmental organizations and charities active in transplantation in Canada, prioritized according to their experience in working directly with living donors on issues of reimbursement—consensus was reached that reimbursing donors for incurred expenses is desirable. Indeed, a comprehensive reimbursement program is being considered in British Columbia, and planning committees working to improve financial support for living donors exist in Alberta, Quebec and Nova Scotia. Most informants held the opinion that existing infrastructure could be used to implement such a program, although additional wherewithal, especially human resources, would be required.

Political, social, regulatory and technical issues may each influence the creation and implementation of a donor reimbursement policy; cost, however, is a major consideration. Although the costs incurred through kidney donation cannot be gauged with certainty, most estimates have ranged from $1,045 to $5,225; in British Columbia, reimbursements to donors are estimated at the midpoint of this range. Allowing for growth in rates of donation, the anticipated annual national costs for such a reimbursement program for living donors of kidneys is $560,000–$2.8 million. In contrast, the cost in 2000 of providing dialysis therapy in Canada was an estimated $9.4 billion. Each kidney donation is expected to save the health care system about $100,000 and provide an additional 2 quality-adjusted life-years. If a 25% overhead for administering a national reimbursement program is assumed, even a 10% increase in kidney donations because of the removal of economic disincentives may result in neutral or net negative costs from a societal perspective.

A National Program
Should Be Implemented

We suggest that a national reimbursement program with federal funding and coordination but provincial implementation would be the best option. The program should include strong safeguards against the commercialization of organs and mechanisms not only for coordinating benefits and adjusting for regional differences in cost of living but also for cost control and promotion of provincial add-ons. Pilot programs would allow a full assessment of the costs and benefits of such a program before widespread implementation, which may allay fears of high program costs.

In conclusion, we rely on altruistically motivated organ donors to improve the health of those with chronic disease. Although we can only strive to attenuate the medical and psychosocial risks associated with donation, it is entirely possible to eliminate the economic risks for Canadian organ donors completely, through legally and ethically acceptable financial reimbursement. Not only is implementation of such a strategy just, but the removal of this barrier is an obvious step to encourage and recognize living donation.

8

Criteria for Defining Death for Organ Donors Should Be More Stringent

John B. Shea

John B. Shea is a retired diagnostic radiologist and a fellow of the Royal College of Canada.

Some in the medical community believe that an individual should be declared dead when they are "brain dead" or "non-heart-beating." In fact, neither "brain-death" nor "non-heart-beating death" criterion clearly indicates that a person has died. Both criteria are scientifically unsound and are applied inconsistently. The demand for organs for transplantation, and the need to secure these organs shortly after a donor's death, may encourage hasty declarations of death under these criteria. The result is that the lives of critically ill but potentially healthy people might unintentionally be sacrificed so that their organs can be taken.

The first heart transplant was performed in 1968. In the same year, the Harvard Ad Hoc Committee declared that a person who was in irreversible coma was, for all practical purposes, though not in reality, dead. That self-contradictory notion of death was immediately adopted by those who promoted organ harvesting and transplantation, and has been used ever since then in an attempt morally to justify these procedures despite the fact that there is still no agreement that the argument is valid.

Criticism in the relevant literature has included the following observations:

1. That the theory is highly controversial and can be used for purely utilitarian purposes.
2. That there is no consensus on diagnostic criteria.
3. That there is evidence of poor compliance with accepted guidelines of 'brain death'.
4. Shewmon has shown that 'brain death' does not lead to the total loss of somatic integrated unity of the bodily functions, the criterion for the death of a person given by Pope John Paul II.

The [Institute of Medicine] found that some teams allowed no time to elapse after the last heart beat or that the time involved was left to the physician's discretion.

'Cardiopulmonary death'

In essence 'brain dead' patients, before their organs are harvested, are assigned the moral status of "heart-beating cadavers." They have become the main source of organs for transplantation over the years. However, the demand for organs increasingly exceeds the supply, so that the number of American patients still in need of organ transplants was more than three times higher than the number of people receiving transplants in the year 2000. This problem of supply and demand has produced pressure from the very beginning in 1968 to find new sources of organs.

In recent years [in the early 2000s], the fiction of 'brain death' has largely been abandoned. Doctors in Calgary suggested that as well as using organs from those who are 'brain dead', organs should also be harvested from patients who are not yet 'brain dead', but in whom the heart has stopped beating.

Already in 1993, a novel way for categorizing patients as dead was conceived. The University of Pittsburgh had developed a protocol, strangely similar in principle to the previous Harvard protocol, which purported to allow patients or their surrogates to offer organs for donation even though the patients were not brain dead. According to the Pittsburgh protocol, if a patient was declared to have suffered irreversible loss of circulatory and respiratory function, he or she was deemed also to have suffered irreversible loss of all brain function, that is to be 'brain dead'. The Institute of Medicine (IOM) found that in so-called "controlled non-heart-beating donation" (NHBD), such a patient would be typically 5 to 55 years old; would have suffered from a severe head injury, but not be 'brain dead'; would not be a drug user or HIV positive; and would be free from hypertension, sepsis or cancer. In other words, this candidate for organ retrieval would, apart from the severe head injury, be young and perfectly well. This patient would also typically be in the emergency department of a hospital and on a ventilator. The decision to declare the patient 'suitable' to donate organs would be made either after, or even before, the withdrawal of life support (ventilation). Discussion between the physicians responsible for the care of the patient and the transplant surgeons would take place before withdrawal of ventilation and, in the majority of cases, before the actual decision to donate organs. Next the ventilation would be withdrawn. The physicians then waited for the heart to stop beating. If the patient was still breathing, they would not wait longer than one hour because, by then, lack of oxygen might have damaged the organs. After an hour the patient would be allowed to die, without treatment being resumed.

In some cases, once the decision to withdraw treatment is made, blood thinners and vessel dilators are given to the patient to help preserve the organs to be transplanted. NHBD promoters say this does not harm the potential donor, but even accidental administration of such medications to an ordinary patient would be a serious error in treatment. If the heart stops beating within an hour of the withdrawal of ventilation, the transplant team usually counts two minutes of pulselessness, and then waits five minutes before removing organs. However, the IOM found that some teams allowed no time to elapse after the last heart beat or that the time involved was left to the physician's discretion.

Standards Vary Depending on Circumstances

The above NHBD procedures are now routinely followed despite the fact that there is no scientific evidence that proves how long after the last heartbeat the heart will no longer be able to start beating again and restore circulation. These procedures are followed also despite the fact that animal studies and cardiopulmonary experience itself show that even complete recovery of consciousness is possible after several minutes if resuscitative efforts are successful. It should be noted that ventilation is treatment that is usually temporary and can be withdrawn after a short period of time when the patient has recovered the ability to breathe without assistance. Traditional ethics allows withdrawal or withholding of treatment which is futile in relation to the survival of the patient, or is excessively burdensome to him or her. It does not allow the withdrawal of ventilation where patient recovery may be possible.

Note also that there are no scientific data to support the notion that a patient has suffered brain death after two minutes of cessation of the heartbeat. What it comes down to is that the transplant team relies on an "expert medical opinion" as to whether the patient has "died." That opinion depends on evidence that the loss of heartbeat was long enough to ensure that the "probability of return of circulatory function is vanishingly small." This time interval, the IOM admits, is not relevant to the determination of death, but will "in a donor with normal body temperature produce irreversible brain damage." That NHBD supporters define death in inconsistent and non-objective terms is demonstrated in a 1999 study of 108 patients. In this study, a potential donor in an intensive care unit who refused resuscitation, was declared "dead" five minutes after cardiopulmonary arrest, according to many NHBD protocols. According to these same protocols, a patient who was willing to undergo resuscitation and was not a donor was not "dead" five minutes after the arrest.

Further, in many intensive care units, a patient who refused resuscitation but was not a potential donor, would be certified "dead" after much less than two minutes, after observation of two or three EKG screens which showed no pulse (about 15–20 seconds). Ambiguity in regard to the terms "irreversible cessation of cardiopulmonary function" was admitted. If "irreversible" means that the heart cannot be restarted no matter what intervention is done, observation for loss of heartbeat, breathing and unresponsiveness must be much longer than a few minutes.

The NHBD Criteria Are Scientifically Unsound

It is evident from the above that the definition of 'death' is not based on objective, scientifically established criteria, but on a variety of protocols, policies, and 'expert medical opinion'. The IOM also admits that a major concern in allowing NHBD is the question as to whether the cardiopulmonary resuscitation of a potential donor has been vigorous or sustained enough. Proponents of the procedure argue that allowing NHBD could increase organ donation by 25%, and go so far as to say that it would also enable patients to determine the point at which they would be declared dead "instead of forcing them to meet brain death criteria. For those who wish to donate organs, but will never meet whole brain death criteria, this also gives meaning to their death."

Critics argue that such protocols would give physicians a perverse incentive to minimize the quality of care given to patients in the hope of harvesting organs, and that the rush to harvest organs shows that physicians are worried that the patient is not really dead; that he or she could regain consciousness during the procedure. Reports and articles supporting NHBD deny that withdrawing ventilation is an ethical problem because the decision to do so is presumed to have been made before the decision to donate is made and independently of it. The dilemma for the patient's physician remains: shall I treat my patient or declare him or her dead and thus benefit some other person by harvesting the organs? The stark reality remains that, as the IOM reported, "controlled non-heart-beating organ donation cannot take place unless life-sustaining treatment is stopped."

The laudable purpose of saving lives does not justify the donation of an organ whose removal could cause the death of the donor.

Despite Problems, NHBD Continues

A follow-up IOM report in the year 2000 found that almost none of its recommendations made about NHBD were being followed universally, and that the participants in the report could not even reach a consensus on such basic issues as to whether conscious people on ventilators should be allowed to donate organs using NHBD. Decisions to withdraw ventilators "are routinely being made because of potential quality of life concerns rather than ability to survive." NHBD proponents nonetheless insist that withdrawal of ventilators is legally and ethically allowable because such patients are regarded as being, in their terms, 'hopeless.'

It will not be surprising if NHBD proponents will push for changes in the law which would allow that death will not be necessary before organ procurement, or for a change in the law that would allow non-heart-beating patients to be defined as 'dead'. Doctors Greg Knoll and John Mahoney have recently encouraged the harvesting of organs by NHBD. They declare that there is an obligation for our health care system in Canada to provide organs and recommend that the use and success of NHBD transplantation "be disseminated to physicians and nurses working in emergency departments, operating rooms, and intensive care units." Patients in those areas of a hospital are presumably regarded as a prime source of organs suitable for transplant.

The NHBD Criteria Threaten Patients' Lives

The laudable purpose of saving lives does not justify the donation of an organ whose removal could cause the death of the donor. The fact is that neither "brain death" criteria nor "non-heart-beating death" criteria definitely indicate that a patient has actually died. As Nancy Valko has pointed out, it is virtually impossible at the beginning of treatment accurately to predict whether a patient will die or what level of recovery he or she may eventually attain. These criteria for defining death are currently being morally defended by a strictly pragmatic and utilitarian ethics, in which the dignity of a human life depends only on the value of its use.

A doubt about the fact concerning the life of a human being, his existence here and now, is a dubium facti [doubt of fact]. As such "it creates the same obligation as certainty." The question as to when a person dies is also a dubium facti, and likewise creates the same obligation as certainty. Pope John Paul II has stated that death "occurs when the spiritual principle which ensures the unity of the individual, can no longer exercise its functions in and upon the organism, whose elements left to themselves, disintegrate." The biologist is the only person competent to say when a human being ceases to exist, and this task has not yet been accomplished.

Organ retrieval based on NHBD criteria is not a boon to humanity, but is yet a further hazard for any critically ill patient, especially if he or she is young and otherwise healthy, who happens to have to cross the threshold of our emergency departments, our operating rooms, or the intensive care units of our hospitals.

9

Better Oversight of the U.S. Transplant System Is Needed

Charles Ornstein and Tracy Weber

Charles Ornstein and Tracy Weber are staff writers for the Los Angeles Times.

The U.S. government contracts with the United Network for Organ Sharing (UNOS) to oversee the organ transplant system. UNOS establishes guidelines for harvesting and allocation of organs and maintains statistical records of outcomes at transplant centers throughout the United States. It is responsible for conducting investigations when problems are reported. Some critics suggest that a basic conflict of interest prevents UNOS from functioning in a regulatory capacity, since it is also a membership organization, made up of practicing transplant surgeons.

The little-known organization that oversees the nation's organ transplant system often fails to detect or decisively fix problems at derelict hospitals—even when patients are dying at excessive rates, a *Times* investigation has found.

When it does act, the United Network for Organ Sharing [UNOS] routinely keeps findings of its investigations secret, leaving patients and their families unaware of the potential risks, interviews and confidential records show.

"It seems like UNOS is often a day late and a dollar short," said Dr. Mark Fox, associate director of the Oklahoma Bioethics Center and former chairman of the UNOS ethics committee. "Most people are kind of shaking their heads and saying, 'Who's minding the store?'"

In the past year [late 2005 into 2006], UNOS has been blindsided by life-threatening lapses at centers it oversees. After the *Times* uncovered such problems at two California programs, both abruptly closed.

UNOS failures in those cases are part of a larger national pattern of uneven and often weak oversight. At times, the group appears more intent on protecting hospitals than patients themselves, the newspaper has found.

Since 1986, the federal government has contracted with UNOS to oversee everything from how organs are harvested to where they end up.

It is a daunting job. The competition for scarce organs is growing. And because the stakes are so high—life or death for patients, prestige and millions of dollars for hospitals—the temptations for transplant centers to bend or break the rules are ever-present.

Reluctant to Act

As the overall arbiter of safety and fairness in the country's transplant system, UNOS has the power to issue public rebukes and urge the government to close troubled programs.

But it has shown itself a reluctant enforcer, according to a *Times* review of confidential UNOS documents and interviews with dozens of past and present board members, transplant doctors, patients and others.

• UNOS has never recommended that the government close an active transplant program.

UNOS leaders say they have been embarrassed to learn about serious failings of their organization in the paper.

Since 2000, the nonprofit organization has considered revoking the "good standing" of at least 15 transplant centers—

its most serious public sanction and a potentially embarrassing blow to a hospital's reputation. But it has followed through just once—in March. In that case, St. Vincent Medical Center in Los Angeles had arranged for a liver transplant candidate to jump ahead of dozens of others in line for an organ.

• Even after programs log high death rates, years sometimes pass before UNOS takes meaningful action.

UNOS, for instance, was aware by 2002 of potentially lethal problems in the kidney program at Sunrise Hospital and Medical Center in Las Vegas, but four years passed before the regulator performed its own inspection. In the meantime, patients were dying at rates UNOS knew to be unacceptably high.

• UNOS often backs down after being challenged—or even defied—by medical centers it is supposed to regulate.

Children's Hospital of Wisconsin in Milwaukee refused UNOS' repeated calls to shut down its lung program in 2004. It wasn't performing any transplants, yet kept children on its waiting list, effectively putting them out of the running for critical surgeries. UNOS threatened its most serious public sanction. The final punishment: confidential probation.

Missing Obvious Problems

• UNOS officials have missed obvious red flags, including troubling transplant center statistics available on its own website.

UNOS statistics showed that Kaiser Permanente's new kidney program in San Francisco was in serious trouble last year [2005]: Twice as many patients had died awaiting transplants as had received them. Other California programs showed the opposite pattern: Twice as many people received transplants as died.

UNOS didn't launch an investigation until May, after the *Times* detailed the program's failings. The program closed that same month.

Celia Scull, 61, said she is angry that UNOS didn't know enough to step in earlier. "I find that appalling," said Scull, a Kaiser transplant candidate from Sacramento who now is transferring to another center. "Does it upset me? You bet it does."

Similarly, UNOS was unaware of the severity of problems within the liver program at UCI Medical Center in Orange [California]. With no full-time surgeon to do transplants for more than a year, UCI turned down scores of organs that might have saved patients on the waiting list. The day the problems were reported in *Times* in November [2005], the program closed.

UNOS leaders say they have been embarrassed to learn about serious failings of their organization in the paper.

Fundamental Problems with the Structure of UNOS

Executive director Walter Graham described the recent troubles at California centers as a "watershed" for UNOS. The problems were "hurting public trust," Graham said. "There has been this escalating desire to stop that. The sense of outrage has grown in the transplant community."

Within the last year, the UNOS board has voted to make some changes, such as publicizing the names of centers on probation and speeding up some investigations. Generally, however, resolving matters amicably serves patients better in the long run than issuing black marks, UNOS officials said.

Such collegiality is built into UNOS' very structure—and that's the problem, some critics say. UNOS isn't just a regulator; it is a membership organization, run mostly by transplant professionals. Centers, in effect, oversee one another.

"UNOS really can't police itself," said Dr. John J. Fung, director of the Cleveland Clinic's transplant center and a former UNOS board member. "Everybody is beholden."

"It's kind of like the fox guarding the chicken house," agreed U.S. Sen. Charles Grassley (R-Iowa), chairman of the Senate Finance Committee, who has ordered an investigation of the country's transplant oversight system by the Government Accountability Office.

In a July 2002 inspection, UNOS found 64 more cases in which the patients' urgent conditions "could not be confirmed with the facts" in their medical records.

"These folks have a short period of time to get their house in order or else they're begging greater government interference and enforcement."

Problems Discovered at Temple University

A few years ago, Temple University Medical Center found a way to speed up its patients' waits for heart transplants.

It reported some patients to be sicker than they were, according to records and interviews, allowing them to jump ahead of patients at other hospitals on a UNOS waiting list.

The hospital did this repeatedly—over four years.

Patients at other hospitals, some of whom were unfairly bumped down the list, had no way of knowing what happened. In fact, the story has never been publicly disclosed.

UNOS knew what was going on, though. In 1999, records show, a UNOS inspection found that the hospital was unable to prove that at least 13 of its patients were sick enough to be classified as "Status 1A," meaning they were on the verge of death and entitled to priority. Temple officials said it was a mistake—it had misinterpreted the rules, according to a confidential UNOS summary of the Temple case.

UNOS closed the matter.

UNOS Does Little to Stop Repeated Offenses

In the months that followed, however, UNOS reviewers determined that Temple had inflated the conditions of 12 more patients. During a January 2001 meeting with UNOS officials, Temple proposed a compromise: It would have its Status 1A listings reviewed in advance by a UNOS panel. In return, the oversight group agreed to hold off on discipline for a year.

In 2002, Temple broke the rules again, misclassifying a patient as near death. After UNOS reviewers rejected the assessment, the hospital proceeded with the transplant anyway.

The hospital's cross-town competitor was incensed.

"If there's a sense that one place isn't playing by the rules, and you play by the rules, then your poor patients aren't going to get a fair shake," Dr. Michael Acker, head of cardiac transplantation at the Hospital of the University of Pennsylvania, said in a recent interview.

In a July 2002 inspection, UNOS found 64 more cases in which the patients' urgent conditions "could not be confirmed with the facts" in their medical records, the UNOS summary said.

That October, UNOS again compromised with Temple, agreeing not to revoke the hospital's "good standing" if Temple promised to change its ways.

The following month, its board of directors placed Temple on confidential probation. Temple completed its probation in January 2006.

"Our transplant program today has been infused with new leadership and improved processes that continue to meet or exceed all recognized industry standards," Temple said in a written statement to the *Times*.

The Children's Hospital of Wisconsin

UNOS' timid response to Temple is not an isolated example.

In 2001, UNOS became aware that the pediatric lung transplant program at Children's Hospital of Wisconsin was performing too few surgeries and had a high death rate, according to a confidential UNOS summary.

UNOS requires hospitals to perform transplants at regular intervals to ensure that patients aren't left waiting in a program that isn't doing them. Separately, Medicare officials set a far higher threshold to make sure a hospital is doing enough procedures to remain proficient.

UNOS also flags programs with inordinate rates of death and organ failure within a year of surgery, based on statistical reports it receives every six months. These data, prepared by a separate government contractor, take into account the condition of patients and organs at individual centers.

In mid-2002, UNOS conducted an inspection at Children's, prompting the hospital to submit a plan to fix its problems.

Another Weak Response by UNOS

About a year and a half later, however, UNOS found the hospital's improvements inadequate. A UNOS disciplinary panel recommended that the program voluntarily suspend itself. Children's refused. The panel asked again in May 2004 and once more in October, with the same result.

Finally, in July 2005, UNOS' disciplinary panel unanimously recommended revoking the program's "good standing," the summary shows.

Two months later, the panel retreated, advocating confidential probation—a decision ultimately approved by the full UNOS board.

The reversal was not explained in the document.

In a statement to the *Times*, Children's defended the program's low numbers, saying the nation's 17 pediatric lung centers performed just 54 transplants last year and that the program has "dedicated significant resources to growing and maintaining expertise."

UNOS officials declined to discuss any of its confidential reviews but suggested the organization is now more aggressive.

"There's no sense in going through that history," said Dr. Francis L. Delmonico, who was UNOS president until June 30. UNOS, he said, has changed. "What may have been in the past—that's a different day."

Judging from the numbers alone, Children's hasn't changed much. As of Friday, it had performed just one transplant in nearly four years.

Six children remain on its waiting list.

UNOS Is Poorly Equipped for Enforcement

Ask current and former UNOS leaders about their enforcement record and they often respond by saying what their organization is not.

"UNOS is not the FBI," said board member Dr. Gabriel Danovitch, medical director of UCLA Medical Center's kidney and pancreas transplant program. "It's not a police force."

"It was never really designed as an enforcement agency," said Dr. Dale Distant, a former board member and transplant chief at SUNY Downstate Medical Center in New York.

In fact, UNOS evolved from a group of transplant professionals who created a computer system in 1977 to ensure that kidneys were fairly distributed.

Few anticipated that by 2005, the nation's 259 transplant centers would perform as many as 28,000 heart, lung, liver, pancreas, kidney and other organ transplants.

Today, UNOS' 276 employees are housed in a sleek, $17.5-million glass complex in Richmond, Va., with an elaborate memorial garden for donors. Each year, it receives $2 million from the federal government and much more—$23 million—in fees from transplant centers.

In 2000, the government gave UNOS more teeth, but the organization prefers to privately nudge centers into compliance.

If all else fails, officials say, they pressure programs to shut themselves down. They say that such pressure has led to the closure—at least temporarily—of more than 80 transplant programs since 2000.

UNOS refused, however, to name the programs or describe the circumstances.

A top federal health official said the government is satisfied with its contractor's performance.

"It ought to be reassuring to people that the vast, vast majority of what's going on is according to good rules that are followed very carefully," said Dr. James Burdick, director of the division of transplantation within the Health Resources and Services Administration.

Burdick is a past president of UNOS.

A Fundamental Conflict

Members of UNOS' board and committees are rotating volunteers—mostly doctors and other transplant professionals who sandwich UNOS duties between other obligations. Some members complain that the group needs more money to handle its growing enforcement needs.

It's a relatively small world in which colleagues—even friends—end up in judgment of one another.

For example, UNOS documents show that at least three of the centers the group is slated to inspect in coming months employ current board members: Vanderbilt University Medical Center in Nashville, Ohio State University Medical Center in Columbus and Christus Santa Rosa Health Care in San Antonio.

Programs at all three have had worse-than-expected surgical outcomes, such as high rates of organ failure or death, based on national statistics.

UNOS says board members must abstain from votes affecting their program or others in their regions. Also, programs are referred to by code during initial inquiries so as not to prejudice opinion. But when discipline is recommended to the full 42-member UNOS board for final approval, the names are revealed.

Judith Braslow, who oversaw the federal government's division of transplantation from 1990 to 1998, said that although UNOS generally does a good job, it is difficult for the group to be "completely objective because they essentially wear two hats."

"In their capacity as the government contractor, they have responsibility to keep the public informed. In their capacity as a membership organization, they have responsibility and loyalty to their members," she said.

"Those two roles are really in conflict in terms of the policing function."

A Deadly Complication

Thomas Pierce, 69, knew nothing of problems at Shands [Hospital] at the University of Florida before his wife's surgery in October 2003. Staffers boasted that the program ranked among "the best there was," Pierce recalled.

In fact, UNOS knew that Shands' kidney patients had been dying at higher-than-expected rates for several years.

After she received her new kidney, Jacqueline Pierce, 60, developed a hernia at the site of her incision and her small bowel became trapped inside of it, a rare complication.

"They said, 'Don't worry, we never lose them,'" Thomas Pierce said. "Then, all of a sudden, I walked in there one day and they said, 'Your wife is going to die.'"

Dr. Peter Stock, a UC San Francisco transplant surgeon who reviewed Jacqueline Pierce's records for the *Times*, said that he could not determine whether her death was avoidable.

Pierce just wishes he had known of Shands' record before he took his wife to the hospital: Statistics monitored by UNOS showed that the hospital had a higher-than-expected death rate dating to 1998. Among patients who received transplants between January 2000 and June 2002, for example, nearly twice as many as expected died within a year. (The statistics cannot be matched to individual patients.)

Today, patient survival has improved at Shands and meets UNOS' standards. Transplant director Dr. Richard Howard said the program has changed the way it selects patients and organs, as well as medication regimens. But Howard, who served on the UNOS board until June and has been at Shands since 1979, said he doesn't recall UNOS' being involved in those reforms.

The center's improvement means nothing to Pierce.

"I can remember driving home from Shands after my wife had died, thinking my life is done," he said. "My wife was my whole life."

No Consistent Backstop

As UNOS has stuck to its slow and silent ways in recent years, other agencies occasionally have stepped in to protect patients or punish wrongdoers.

In 2002, for instance, the federal government was forced to sue UNOS—its own contractor—to get information about allegedly improper conduct by three liver transplant programs in Chicago. UNOS argued the information was confidential.

A federal judge sided with the government, saying that the material could show "whether some [patients] have been permitted to barge to the head of the line."

The hospitals later agreed to settle federal claims alleging that they had fraudulently diagnosed and hospitalized certain patients to make them eligible for transplants sooner.

More recently, the UNOS board took no public action against three transplant centers in New York, even though state officials found problems egregious enough to levy fines.

In 2004, for example, regulators fined Strong Memorial Hospital in Rochester [New York] $20,000 for failing to document why the liver transplant program was using less-than-ideal organs and not telling patients about the risks. At least two patients suffered organ failure and needed new transplants.

In a statement at the time, Dr. Antonia C. Novello, New York's health commissioner, said she was "troubled by the gaps in the hospital's quality assurance system" and its failure to "correct significant breakdowns in its liver transplant program."

It is not clear whether UNOS was aware of these problems. But it had considered revoking Strong's "good standing" the previous year—in that case, for exaggerating the conditions of its heart and liver patients. It ultimately didn't do so, records show.

Despite these cases, UNOS generally has no consistent backstop if it fails to do its job.

The U.S. Centers for Medicare and Medicaid Services oversees the nation's federally funded transplant centers—a significant part of the system. The two organizations' regulatory duties overlap somewhat. Both, for instance, are supposed to keep an eye on death rates. But they rarely have shared information and have different standards for flagging errant programs.

One characteristic they often share: failing to act decisively.

According to a *Times* investigation in June, the Medicare agency had neglected to pull funding from nearly 50 programs that did not meet its minimum standards in recent years.

High Rate of Failure at Sunrise Hospital

Among the programs given years of leeway by UNOS, the kidney transplant center at Sunrise Hospital and Medical Center in Las Vegas stands out.

Sunrise, just a few minutes' drive from the city's famed Strip, first heard of the regulator's concerns in 2002, a hospital official said. UNOS sent a matter-of-fact letter noting the center's high incidence of organ failure after transplants and asking for more information.

UNOS knew that between July 1998 and June 2000, 21% of the transplanted kidneys failed within a year, more than twice the expected rate of 9%. The program's survival rate was low as well: 88% for patients one year after surgery, compared with an expected 95%, given its patients' conditions. Over the next four years, patients continued to die at excessive rates. But UNOS appeared locked in a slow procedural dance, based on its internal records.

It recommended an inspection in January 2003, then put it "on hold" so that Sunrise could bring in its own outside reviewer, internal UNOS documents show.

That review found that program officials were "not as stringent as [they] should have been" in weeding out patients who were not good transplant candidates, in particular older patients with heart disease, Dr. Scott A. Slavis, Sunrise's medical director and sole surgeon, said earlier this year [2006]. In response, the program changed its criteria for new patients, Slavis said.

But too many patients continued to die.

The 2003 reforms, said Amy Stevens, system vice president for Sunrise Health, "didn't close the gap enough between expected and actual deaths."

In April 2005, a UNOS panel recommended that the group do its own inspection within "the next three to six months," records show. Nearly a year passed before UNOS reviewers finally went to Sunrise. All the while, Sunrise remained a member of UNOS "in good standing."

"We never heard anything about that," said Janis Alamo, referring to Sunrise's death rates. "We didn't know any of that."

Alamo's husband, Delfino, was on Sunrise's kidney waiting list for more than two years before he transferred to the city's other program because, she said, he found staff members difficult.

Deaths Continue While UNOS Does Little

In fact, as the UNOS inquiry dragged on, Sunrise's survival rates remained among the lowest in the country in 10 consecutive statistical reports, updated every six months. No other transplant program had a lower-than-expected rate for so long.

About 15 more patients died than expected within a year of their surgeries between 2000 and 2004, according to these statistics. It is an extreme number for a program performing about 30 surgeries a year.

Stevens said the hospital is addressing UNOS' concerns. It is recruiting a second transplant surgeon and has filed a detailed plan of correction.

"We are committed to building this program," she said.

Stevens said the program never directly told patients about the problems but provided them with website addresses that would allow them to view outcome statistics.

Patients and transplant specialists say such statistics are often incomprehensible to the layperson. Monitoring the numbers—and stepping in where necessary—is UNOS' job.

"I think they've done a disservice to the patients at that program that are waiting," said the Cleveland Clinic's Fung when told of UNOS' handling of the Sunrise situation.

UNOS officials declined to comment specifically on Sunrise. Dr. Sue V. McDiarmid, UNOS' president, said it is better for the group's investigations to be thorough than quick.

"If you come down too fast and hurriedly and potentially wrongly, you can do a good deal of harm to patients on the waiting list," said McDiarmid, who also is a pediatric liver specialist at UCLA Medical Center.

For the last four years, the dozens of patients on Sunrise's waiting list have been none the wiser.

10

The Involuntary Harvesting of Organs Is a Crime Against Humanity

Wang Wenyi

Naturalized U.S. citizen and activist Wang Wenyi trained as a physician in China, earned a PhD in pharmacology from the University of Chicago, and completed a residency in pathology at New York's Mount Sinai Hospital. In April of 2006 she was arrested and charged with a misdemeanor after attempting to disrupt a speech by visiting Chinese president Hu Jintao, in order to protest the harvesting of organs from living Falun Gong prisoners in China.

Falun Gong is a spiritual movement that is being repressed by the Chinese Communist Party (CCP) that runs the government of China. Tens of thousands of Falun Gong practitioners are held as political prisoners in Chinese labor camps. These prisoners are the source of organs being sold to foreigners, who come to China because they are told that organs can be found and transplanted into them on short notice. It is a crime against humanity to dissect people for their organs. This cruel and inhumane practice amounts to genocide and should not be allowed to continue. I disrupted the press conference of presidents Bush and Jintao to bring attention to this issue, which is largely ignored by the media.

Wang Wenyi, "A Cry to Awaken Our Conscience," *The Epoch Times International*, April 24, 2006. Copyright © 2000–2006 Epoch Times International. Reproduced by permission.

I was released from the D.C. District Court on Friday, April 21 [2006]. I think it is necessary for me to give the public an explanation for my protest during Hu Jintao's [the president of China] remarks Thursday morning on the south lawn of the White House.

On March 9 *The Epoch Times* reported the large-scale organ removal from living Falun Gong [a movement that the Chinese government suppresses] practitioners' in the Sujiatun District, Shenyang City, Liaoning Province in northeastern China. After this story broke, the Chinese Communist Party (CCP) [the CCP rules China] quickly transferred the Falun Gong practitioners still held in the Sujiatun area, took other steps to cover up what had been done, and denied the incident. At this time, *The Epoch Times* assigned me to follow this story because I am a pathologist and have experience in organ transplant research.

Transplant doctors in China have openly admitted in tape-recorded phone calls that the organs are from living Falun Gong practitioners.

Initially our story was based on the accounts of two individuals from the Shenyang area with information about what had happened inside the hospitals in Sujiatun: "Peter," a Chinese national who had worked as a producer for a Japanese TV station in the Shenyang City area; and "Annie," who was a staff member at the Liaoning Provincial Thrombosis Hospital of Integrated Chinese and Western Medicine and the former wife of a surgeon who had performed organ harvesting at Sujiatun for several years.

From the beginning of March, I have been accompanying these two sources to interviews with major international media, the members of the U.S. Congress, and governmental agencies. At the same time, we obtained information regarding large-scale organ harvesting from living Falun Gong practitioners between 2001 and 2003 in major labor camps that detained Falun Gong practitioners.

Political Prisoners Are Being Killed to Supply Organs

Everyone associated with this scheme who withdraws from it puts his or her life at risk.

Some patients who had gone to China for organ transplant operations told us that they were told prior to their going to China that the organ sources were Falun Gong practitioners. Some doctors who know the overall picture of the live organ harvesting scheme told us the cruelty and inhumanity is unthinkable, unspeakable and far beyond what has been reported in *The Epoch Times*. They told us that when the scheme was completely exposed, people around the world would be stunned.

Two witnesses who risked their lives to expose the organ removal from living Falun Gong practitioners were not allowed to explain what they knew.

Although these people have been in close contact with *The Epoch Times*, they dare not step forward because they are afraid of being killed. They all closely follow the issue and in particular the stance of the U.S. government and the international media because they need a safe environment.

I realized that it is very important for the U.S. government to know about this. I have been constantly providing contacts in the government updated information.

Patients require living healthy organs. In order to attract business, transplant doctors in China have openly admitted in tape-recorded phone calls that the organs are from living Falun Gong practitioners. In addition, almost all hospitals make public statements that the waiting time for suitable organs range from two weeks to a month. Sometimes it takes only a week to complete the process of finding an organ, blood and tissue matching and transplantation.

The multi-language online advertisement of an organ transplant center in Shenyang even promised that in 3 weeks patients can go to China, complete organ transplantation and resume work happily. After the Sujiatun news broke, the Chinese Web page of this organ transplant was removed. As a doctor with a background in organ transplantation, I clearly know that there must be large-scale live-organ banks in many provinces in Mainland China. I feel great pain at the thought of this.

We have tens of thousands of missing Falun Gong practitioners. Their families search for them, but have no clue at all as to their whereabouts.

Harvesting Continues Under a Cover-Up

I want to emphasize to the public what is happening right now. A lot of investigation, including recorded interviews with transplant doctors in China, indicates that major hospitals in China are performing operations at this very time to remove organs from living Falun Gong practitioners. Our investigations also show that hospitals in China are hastening to perform these operations as quickly as possible.

Soon after the news of organ harvesting from living Falun Gong practitioners came out, the CCP issued a new directive regarding organ transplantation. Although the directive appears to outlaw the organ harvesting that has been taking place, it does not go into effect until July 1 [2006]. Meanwhile, many hospitals are urging patients to have organ transplantation done soon. They have said that the organ sources will be not so abundant after May 1. Recordings documenting these claims have been published online.

It is obvious that the Chinese Communist Party is covering things up, and at the same time, rushing to complete organ transplants as quickly as possible. We know that every single day large numbers of Falun Gong practitioners are being sacrificed to provide the necessary organs.

I haven't had time for my children. I left them in New York. I have been visiting various governmental agencies and media. I hope to immediately stop the crimes of organ harvesting from living Falun Gong practitioners and to rescue those facing the danger of live organ removal.

When I talked to the media, some media representatives told me that they believed organ removal from living human beings was true. However, because the media couldn't handle the pressure or didn't want to affect the bilateral relationship between their countries and China, they couldn't report on this.

The Reason I Cried Out

On April 19, the day before the meeting between President Bush and Hu Jintao, I went to a congressional hearing about human rights in China. However, the two witnesses who risked their lives to expose the organ removal from living Falun Gong practitioners were not allowed to explain what they knew. At the time, the two witnesses had only requested that they be allowed to testify in private before the Congressmen. After they saw that the hearing did not have any testimony about what they knew was true, they bravely decided to make their first public statements at a press conference held on April 21.

I believe the live organ removal is the most severe crime against humanity, the most severe and most large-scale genocide happening right now—right in front of our eyes.

After this congressional hearing, I realized I had to do whatever I could to call attention to the organ harvesting from living Falun Gong practitioners. On April 20, I went to the White House to report. However, when I saw President Bush shake hands with Hu Jintao, I couldn't help but cry out.

I cried out for those Falun Gong practitioners, for those who have been or are going to be dissected alive for their organs. I cried out for those who have been tortured and suffered genocidal persecution.

I don't want the U.S. president and the international media to be deceived by the CCP any more. I hope that Hu Jintao does not follow Jiang Zemin [his predecessor as president] in the persecution and genocide of Falun Gong.

I have been trying to tell the facts of this persecution to our readers and the public. I have been attending and covering many international events. I believe the live organ removal is the most severe crime against humanity, the most severe and most large-scale genocide happening right now—right in front of our eyes.

Organ Harvesting Is a Crime Against Humanity that Must Be Stopped

Live organ harvesting is a crime that all of humankind ought to join together to end. The information about this issue has been repeatedly covered up. I had no choice but to adopt this means to expose it.

I acted in a way consistent with the American spirit. I also acted to protect the dignity of America and humankind.

Afterwards, I was detained for a day. When I was released, I saw many media waiting for me in front of the courthouse. They all asked me, "Why?"

Since released I have given interviews to the press. Right before one interview with a major international media company, in the elevator as we rode up together, the show's producer clearly told me not to mention organs. Information about large-scale organ harvesting from living Falun Gong practitioners has been covered up these past six weeks.

The press reported what I did at the White House, but did not report very much about the reason why I acted. However, why I acted is the key to the whole issue.

America is America because of its high respect for human rights. I think the massive organ removal from living Falun Gong practitioners touches and challenges the conscience of each one of us. It is a challenge for humankind. Such crimes and sins should not be allowed to continue.

11

Condemned Prisoners Should Not Be Considered as Organ Donors

UNOS Ethics Committee

The United Network for Organ Sharing (UNOS) is a non-profit, scientific and educational organization that administers the nation's only Organ Procurement and Transplantation Network (OPTN). It was established by the U.S. Congress in 1984.

The growing demand for organs for transplantation has led to suggestions that organs might be recovered from prisoners who have been sentenced to death. However, the death penalty itself is controversial and is, in fact, not employed in any industrialized country with the exception of the United States. It would be very difficult to ensure that any condemned prisoner's decision to donate organs was coercion free. The UNOS Ethics Committee opposes organ donation from condemned prisoners until ethical concerns have been addressed.

As the scarcity of suitable organs for transplantation continues to grow, alternative sources for organs have been reported and others suggested. One such suggestion is to recover organs that would otherwise seem to go to waste, such as those from condemned prisoners. Reportedly the People's Republic of China recovers organs from executed prisoners, and recent U.S. news reports have alleged that organ brokers operate in this country who arrange transplantation of the foreign prisoners' organs. This discussion is not restricted to third world countries. In the United States, proposals of this type have come from prominent figures and bodies. While one proposal suggested that prisoners be given the option of donating organs upon their death, another suggests that condemned prisoners be offered the option of trading a kidney or their bone marrow in exchange for a commuted sentence of life in prison without parole.

While it is beyond the scope of the UNOS Ethics Committee to examine the moral and ethical issues encompassing the death penalty, it is worth noting that this topic is both ethically and judicially controversial. Acknowledgment should at least be made that the death penalty is rarely available or applied in most industrialized western nations, except for the United States. All western European countries, Canada, Mexico, Central and South American, with the exception of Chile, have abolished the death penalty. Recent U.S. data show an inequitable application of the death penalty with a significant evidence of racial bias particularly in the South. The data indicate that blacks are five times more likely to be sentenced to death than whites convicted of similar crimes and that the economically disadvantaged as well are more likely than the wealthy to receive the death penalty.

Serious Ethical Issues

Any law or proposal that allows a person to trade an organ for a reduction in sentence, particularly a sentence from death to life in prison, raises numerous issues. Application of the death penalty is spasmodic and seemingly discriminatorily applied, which would suggest that these types of proposals would be coercive to particular classes of individuals—minorities and the poor. Would the reduction in sentence apply to the offer to donate, or would it only be honored if the act of donation took place? If the act of donation would exclusively qualify for the reduction in sentence, then the law or policy would discriminate against individuals found to be medically unsuitable to donate organs. Examples include:

- those with common prison infections such as tuberculosis, HIV or hepatitis B

- the prisoners with a single functioning kidney, or on dialysis, or with diabetes or other renal diseases

Were prisoners allowed to trade a kidney to mitigate a death sentence, it may affect the actual imposition of the death penalty. With greater publicity surrounding these types of proposals/laws, potential jurors could be influenced and ultimately impose the death penalty more often with a potential societal benefit in mind. Jurors might hope that the convicted persons would choose to trade their kidney for their life. This would present a gross inequity for those unable or unwilling to donate a kidney and who might otherwise have not received a death sentence.

Obviously a person condemned to death cannot consider organ or bone marrow donation as a coercion-free option.

The proposals that concern organ recovery from executed prisoners unveil another host of problems. One method of execution suggested is the act of organ donation itself. From a utilitarian standpoint this would make sense; the anesthetizing of the condemned and the recovery of organs in the usual manner would produce optimum organs for transplantation. However, the cross-clamping the aorta and the ensuing cardiectomy, followed by the disconnection of the ventilator, create an unacceptable situation for the organ recovery team. It clearly places the organ recovery team in the role of executioner. Many physician groups, including the American Medical Association, have prohibited physician participation in state executions on ethical grounds.

Issues of informed consent of potential donors as well as recipients need to be addressed. Obviously a person condemned to death cannot consider organ or bone marrow donation as a coercion-free option. Even a death row inmate should have the option of refusing an invasive surgical procedure—although unlikely, given the alternative. Correspondingly a person to be executed, or their next of kin/surrogate, should be able to make an informed decision regarding any donation options, including informed refusal if they so chose. Ultimately the potential organ/bone marrow recipient(s) should be informed that the source of the donation was a condemned prisoner, while maintaining the prisoner's confidentiality. Individuals in opposition to the death penalty might object to accepting an organ from either an executed prisoner or a prisoner who traded their organ for their life.

Potential for Negative Consequences

Consider the effect that such a policy/law could have on organ donation overall. The number of potential organs recovered from condemned prisoners would be small. The conceivable stigma that would be attached to organ donation from its coupling with execution could lead to decreases in donation rates. This may especially be true within certain minority groups. Any notion that particular groups of people were receiving increased numbers of death sentences to provide organs for the rest of society would clearly make it difficult to attempt to obtain consent for altruistic donation from these groups.

Conclusion The UNOS Ethics Committee has raised a small number of the many issues regarding organ donation from condemned prisoners. The Committee opposes any strategy or proposed statute regarding organ donation from condemned prisoners until all of the potential ethical concerns have been satisfactorily addressed.

12

Convicts Should Not Be Automatically Excluded from Receiving Transplants

W. Victoria Lee

W. Victoria Lee wrote this article while she was on the staff of The Tech, *a student publication of the Massachusetts Institute of Technology.*

When a California convict died a few months after receiving a $2 million taxpayer-funded heart transplant, serious questions were raised about the allocation of scarce organs. Legislation was introduced to prevent condemned prisoners from receiving donated organs, after reports surfaced of angry Californians tearing up their organ donor cards. But decisions about who should receive available organs should not be driven by impulsive emotion and stereotypes. Instead, each person should be considered as an individual.

Imagine you die in a car accident. Because you are a rational and generous citizen, you have indicated an organ donation on your driver's license. Doctors remove all your usable organs, including your heart. This heart, still warm, is immediately prepared for transport to another hospital where a patient is getting ready to receive it. Watching this from above, you smile and are glad that your misfortune has turned into someone else's fortune. This patient is no different from the other 80,000 patients in the nation on the waiting list for an

W. Victoria Lee, "A New Heart, or Liver, For a Convict." *The Tech*, January 29, 2003. Reproduced by permission.

organ transplant: bed-ridden, dying, and desperate. The only thing that might set him apart from the others is that he is an inmate, a man who has committed unforgivable deeds against our society. Would you still be smiling?

But then imagine yourself as an inmate who is currently serving a sentence for crimes committed during your youth. You have since resolved to be a better person and are looking forward to your imminent eligibility for parole. The only thing that stands in your way is your failing heart. You are told that you need a new heart, but you are also told that you will be placed on a separate waiting list, a list just for inmates. Patients on this list can only pray that someone among the one-third of the people who die with reusable body parts is willing to give his or her organs to an inmate. Would you consider this discrimination, or a violation of human rights?

Where do we draw the line as to whom the donated organs should go? We don't. Erase the line, forget the yes-no options, and treat it case by case.

Difficult Choices

You probably have not pondered these questions yet; neither did I until recently. A Californian convict, the first inmate to receive a heart transplant while serving his 14-year sentence for robbery, died a few months after his $2 million taxpayer-funded surgery and medical care. Outraged by this "waste" of the otherwise perfectly reusable heart and money, and inspired by his father's death while waiting for a liver transplant, California State Sen. Jeff Denham proposed a bill to give California organ donors the freedom to decide that their organs not go to inmates. He argued that donors would like to know that their deaths have brought lives to those who will contribute to society, and not to those behind bars who have not only failed at that task but have instead brought harm. Denham recently told the *Los Angeles Times* that he had reports of angry Californians tearing up their organ donor cards upon discovering the state-funded transplant.

Indeed, would you want to give your organs to an ax murderer or child molester? Some would say keeping organs from inmates is inhuman, that the prisoners are human, too, and that they deserve organ transplants just like other patients do. However, we take away prisoners' ability to vote and other rights held by most citizens, and nobody is jumping up and down denouncing the inhumanity of such punishment.

Until 1996, every patient who needed an organ transplant was placed on the same waiting list. After the former "Dallas" star Larry Hagman received a new liver, outrage brought the United Network for Organ Sharing to the decision that people who require liver transplant due to excessive use of alcohol and drugs will not be placed on top of the waiting list. Such restriction has happened before, and it might happen again. In the USA, every 90 minutes a patient dies waiting for an organ transplant. How do we decide who gets the next available organ? A spokeswoman for the California Transplant Donor Network answered this question in a *Los Angeles Times* article: "organ allocation system is based solely on medical and scientific criteria, not on which patient is the richest, the smartest or the most socially acceptable." Fair enough. But can we choose to whom we want to give our organs? After all, the organs are ours.

Each Case Should Be Judged on Its Own Merits

It is assumed that when we signed up to become organ donors we expressed our wish to help the patient who most needed the organ, and doctors can accurately and fairly determine who needs an organ most. The real problem is deciding who most deserves the organ. How do we determine whether one life is more worthy than another? Just because one is imprisoned does not necessarily mean that he or she is more morally corrupted than a free businessman who embezzles and deceives. Is a robber who takes good care of his elderly parents more immoral than a politician who lies to the public and neglects his family? Wrongful accusations and undeserved freedom happen; we cannot give an accurate moral judgment of people based on one or two events in which they have participated. On the other hand, it is not so practical to invest the gift of an organ and to spend millions of taxpayers' money on a serial killer sentenced to life or even an inmate who is on death row. Of course, the possibilities that these prisoners have been wrongfully accused and the real criminals are running free exist. In a real world where anything is possible one can only work with what one knows, but significant effort should be made to ensure the final decision is not driven by impulsive emotion and stereotypes.

Not every inmate deserves a second chance to live and not every immoral, undeserving person is behind bars. Where do we draw the line as to whom the donated organs should go? We don't. Erase the line, forget the yes-no options, and treat it case by case.

13

Animal-to-Human Transplants Carry the Risk of Spreading Diseases

Luis Fabregas

Luis Fabregas is a staff writer for the Pittsburgh Tribune-Review.

Researchers are exploring the possibility of developing pig organs suitable for transplant into humans. However, organizations such as the Campaign for Responsible Transplantation, have lobbied against animal-to-human transplants. They are concerned about the possibility that animal diseases could be transferred, unwittingly infecting not only transplant patients, but also their families and healthcare workers.

The potential of pig-to-human organ transplants begs the question: Could a pig organ transfer deadly animal viruses into humans?

That's been the top worry among critics of the controversial field of cross-species transplantation.

Their worries are justified. Pigs carry a virus known as porcine endogenous virus, or PERV. The virus, which some have likened to HIV, can infect human cells in the laboratory, according to British scientists.

But recent studies have shown PERV to be less of a threat than previously thought.

In 2004 scientists at Harvard Medical School transplanted human and pig cells into mice. After six months, tests showed PERV did not infect the human cells.

Luis Fabregas, "Animal Viruses: A Risk for Humans," *Pittsburgh Tribune-Review*, April 9, 2006. Copyright © 2006 Tribune-Review Publishing Co. Reproduced by permission.

Still, the possibility of PERV or other viruses crossing species has weighed heavily on some groups.

The Campaign for Responsible Transplantation, based in New York, has lobbied forcefully against animal-to-human transplants. In 2000, it filed a lawsuit against the U.S. Food and Drug Administration, demanding documents on the side effects and deaths caused by human xenotransplantation [transplants from animals] trials.

The lawsuit produced several thousand documents that are still [as of 2006] being reviewed by the group.

Some documents have shown that some xenotransplantation patients developed side effects such as tumors, says Alix Fano, the group's executive director.

"You can't make this technology safe at all," Fano says.

The public needs the reassurance of the scientists that the organs are safe.

Fano's group worries that placing pig cells and organs in humans will foster the transmission of PERV and other unknown animal diseases they believe could remain dormant for years.

"Whatever you do, those (pig) cells carry the risk of infection not only to the patients, but their relatives and their health care workers. The pigs are laden with retroviruses, and we don't know all of them. In my mind, it's extremely dangerous and irresponsible," she says.

More Research Is Necessary

The transmission of animal diseases also has worried members of an advisory committee for the U.S. Department of Health and Human Services.

"You can't know for sure whether or not you are going to introduce an infectious disease through xenotransplantation," Dr. Jonathan S. Allan of the Southwest Foundation for Biomedical Research in San Antonio, said at the committee's last meeting in February 2004, according to meeting transcripts. "To suggest there is no risk, I don't think anybody would suggest there is no risk."

The advisory committee was disbanded in January after five years because there had been little activity in the field.

Dr. Sharon C. Kiely, a Pittsburgh internist who sat on the committee, says xenotransplantation will have difficulty moving forward unless tests show more consistent survival among those getting the organs.

"The public needs the reassurance of the scientists that the organs are safe," says Kiely, vice chairwoman of the department of medicine at Allegheny General Hospital in the North Side. "The public health implications are unknown. Whenever there's a new frontier, we need to be sure this is consistent with the public health culture of this country."

David Ayares, the president and chief executive officer of Revivicor, the biotech firm cloning pigs for xenotransplantation, says the company has talked with U.S. Food and Drug Administration officials about the matter.

All organs, he says, would be tested for PERV before they are transplanted.

Organizations to Contact

The editors have compiled the following list of organizations concerned with the issues debated in this book. The descriptions are derived from materials provided by the organizations. All have publications or information available for interested readers. The list was compiled on the date of publication of the present volume; the information provided here may change. Be aware that many organizations take several weeks or longer to respond to inquiries, so allow as much time as possible.

American Organ Transplant Association (AOTA)
21175 Tomball Parkway, Ste. 194, Houston, Texas   77070
(713) 344–2402
Web site: http://www.aotaonline.org/

AOTA is a nonprofit organization that works to remove financial obstacles and make transplant surgery available to anyone who needs it. It provides assistance with fundraising and also provides financial support to help with travel expenses and the cost of drugs.

American Society of Transplant Surgeons (ASTS)
2461 South Clark St., Ste 640, Arlington, VA   22202
(703) 414–7870
Web site: www.asts.org

ASTA is an organization of surgeons, physicians, and other scientists who are actively engaged in organ transplantation. Its purpose is to support education and research about organ and tissue transplantation to facilitate the saving of lives and to enhance the quality of life of patients afflicted with end-stage organ failure. It publishes the *American Journal of Transplantation* and posts statements about ethics and public policy on its Web site.

Campaign for Responsible Transplantation (CRT)

PO Box 2751, New York, NY   10163–2751

(212) 579–3477

Web site: www.crt-online.org

CRT is a non-profit organization launched in 1998 out of concern over the rush to commercialize animal-to-human organ transplantation (xenotransplantation), using genetically modified pigs and non-human primates. CRT believes that xenotransplantation poses a grave danger to human health because of the risk of transferring deadly animal viruses to the human population. News updates, press releases, and other resources are available on the CRT Web site.

Center for Bioethics

University of Pennsylvania, Philadelphia, PA   19104

(215) 898–7136

Web site http://www.bioethics.upenn.edu/

The Center for Bioethics is an academic program of the University of Pennsylvania. Its members teach, engage in research, and publish many articles about the ethics of organ transplantation. *PennBioethics* is its quarterly newsletter.

The Hastings Center

21 Malcolm Gordon Road, Garrison, NY   10524–4125

(914) 424–4040

Web site: http://www.thehastingscenter.org/

The Hastings Center is an independent research institute that explores emerging questions in medicine, health care, and biotechnology.

International Society for Heart and Lung Transplantation (ISHLT)

14673 Midway Road, Ste. 200, Addison, TX   75001

(972) 490–9495

Web site: www.ishlt.org

ISHLT is a not-for-profit organization of scientists and medical professionals who specialize in research on or treatment of end-stage heart and lung diseases. The society publishes a newsletter and the *Journal of Heart and Lung Transplantation*.

LifeSharers
6509 Cornwall Dr., Nashville, TN   37205
Web site: http://www.lifesharers.org/

LifeSharers is a non-profit organization that seeks to increase the number of organs available for transplant and, in its opinion, make the system for allocating organs more fair. LifeSharers believes that people who promise to donate their own organs upon their death should be first in line to receive organ transplants should they need them while they are alive. Members of LifeSharers have agreed that when they die, their organs will go to other LifeSharers members if they need them or to the general population if no LifeSharers member requires them.

National Foundation for Transplants (NFT)
5350 Poplar Ave., Ste. 430, Memphis, TN   38119
(800) 489–3863
Web site: www.transplants.org

The NFT is a non-profit organization whose mission is to help those in need of organ transplants pay for them. It helps with fundraising and provides assistance in paying for the cost of medical procedures and drugs not covered by insurance.

National Kidney Foundation (NKF)
30 East Thirty-third Street, New York, NY   10016
(800) 622–9010
Web site: www.kidney.org

The NKF is a health organization dedicated to combating kidney disease. Kidneys are among the organs most commonly transplanted, and part of the NKF's mission is to educate the public about all types organ transplants. The NKF maintains a number of programs related to organ donation and transplantation and is a prominent public voice on these issues.

TransWeb
The Northern Brewery, Ann Arbor, MI   48105
Web site: www.transweb.org

TransWeb is a non-profit organization based at the University of Michigan that maintains an educational Web site serving the world transplant community. TransWeb features news and events, real people's experiences, the top ten myths about donation, a donation quiz, and a large collection of questions and answers, as well as a reference area with everything from articles to videos.

Uncaged Campaigns
9 Bailey Lane, Sheffield, U.K.   S1 4EG
+44 (0) 114 272 2220
Web site: www.uncaged.co.uk

Uncaged Campaigns is an animal rights organization based in the United Kingdom. Its members oppose animal-to-human transplants on scientific and ethical grounds and promote vegan, feminist, and green philosophies.

United Network for Organ Sharing (UNOS)
PO Box 13770, Richmond, VA   23225
(804) 330-8500
Web site: www.unos.org

UNOS is a system of transplant and organ procurement centers, tissue-typing labs, and transplant surgical teams. It was formed to help organ donors and people who need organs to find each other. By federal law, organs used for transplants in the United States must be cleared through UNOS. The network also formulates and implements national policies on equal access to organs and organ allocation, organ procurement, and AIDS testing. It publishes the monthly *UNOS Update.*

Bibliography

Books

American Medical Association Family Medical Guide. Hoboken, NJ: John Wiley & Sons, 2004.

Robert E. Adler *Medical Firsts: From Hippocrates to the Human Genome.* Hoboken, NJ: John Wiley & Sons, 2004.

Annie Cheney *Body Brokers: Inside America's Underground Trade in Human Remains.* New York: Broadway Books, 2006.

Mark J. Cherry *Kidney for Sale by Owner: Human Organs, Transplantation, and the Market.* Washington DC: Georgetown University Press, 2005.

D.K.C. Cooper *Xeno: The Promise of Transplanting Animal Organs into Humans.* New York: Oxford University Press, 2000.

Cecile Fabre *Whose Body Is It Anyway?: Justice and the Integrity of the Person.* New York: Oxford University Press, 2006.

Michele Goodwin *Black Markets: The Supply and Demand of Body Parts.* New York: Cambridge University Press, 2006.

Sue Holtkamp *Wrapped in Mourning: The Gift of Life and Organ Donor Family Trauma.* New York: Brunner-Routledge, 2002.

Joseph H. Howell and William F. Sale — *Life Choices: A Hastings Center Introduction to Bioethics.* Washington, DC: Georgetown University Press, 2000.

Albert R. Jonsen — *Bioethics Beyond the Headlines: Who Lives? Who Dies? Who Decides?* Lanham, MD: Rowman & Littlefield, 2005.

David L. Kaserman and A.H. Barnett — *The U.S. Organ Procurement System: A Prescription for Reform.* Washington, DC: AEI Press, 2002.

Tom Koch — *Scarce Goods: Justice, Fairness and Organ Transplantation.* Westport, CT: Praeger, 2002.

Margaret M. Lock — *Twice Dead: Organ Transplants and the Reinvention of Death.* Berkeley: University of California Press, 2002.

Ronald Munson — *Raising the Dead: Organ Transplants, Ethics and Society.* New York: Oxford University Press, 2002.

Elizabeth Parr and Janet Mize — *Coping with an Organ Transplant: A Practical Guide to Understanding, Preparing for and Living with an Organ Transplant.* New York: Avery, 2001.

Jodi Picoult — *My Sister's Keeper: A Novel.* New York: Atria, 2004.

David J. Rothman and Sheila M. Rothman — *Trust Is Not Enough: Bringing Human Rights to Medicine.* New York: New York Review Books, 2006.

Joyce Brennfleck Shannon	*Transplantation Sourcebook: Basic Consumer Health Information About Organ and Tissue Transplantation.* Detroit, MI: Omnigraphics, 2002.
Wesley J. Smith	*Culture of Death: The Assault on Medical Ethics in America.* San Francisco: Encounter Books, 2000.
James Stacey Taylor	*Stakes and Kidneys: Why Markets in Human Body Parts Are Morally Imperative.* Burlington, VT: Ashgate Publications, 2005.
Nicholas L. Tilney	*Transplant: From Myth to Reality.* New Haven, CT: Yale University Press, 2003.
Robert M. Veatch	*Transplantation Ethics.* Washington, DC: Georgetown University Press, 2000.
Tyler Volk	*What Is Death?: A Scientist Looks at the Cycle of Life.* New York: John Wiley & Sons, 2002.
Stephen Wilkinson	*Bodies for Sale: Ethics and Exploitation in the Human Body Trade.* New York: Routledge, 2003.
Stuart J. Youngner and Martha W. Anderson	*Transplanting Human Tissue: Ethics, Policy, and Practice.* New York: Oxford University Press, 2004.

Periodicals

Jerry Adler	"A Tragic Error," *Newsweek*, March 3, 2003.

Marsha Austin "Activists Defend Private Deals to Match Organ Donor, Recipient; Transplant Advocates Say They Support Methods That Save Lives but Oppose Buying and Selling Parts," *Denver Post*, October 26, 2004.

Tresa Baldas "Proposed Organ Removal Law Raises Legal Concerns," *The Recorder*, July 14, 2006.

Jody A. Charnow "Transplant Tourist Beware: Going to Another Country for a Kidney May Shorten Wait, But Hike Risks," *Renal & Urology News*, July 2006.

Lloyd R. Cohen and David J. Undis "New Solution to the Organ Shortage: Is There a Simple and Better Incentive to Increase Organ Donations," *Saturday Evening Post*, March–April, 2006.

Robert Davis "Online Organ Match Raises Ethical Concerns," *USA Today*, October 26, 2004.

Sigrid Fry-Revere "A Federal Organ Grab," *New York Post*, November 2, 2006.

Bruce Jancin "Reassessing Living-Donor Liver Transplantation," *Internal Medicine News*, May 1, 2003.

Unmesh Kher and Paul Cuadros "A Miracle Denied," *Time*, March 3, 2003.

C.D. Kirkpatrick and Jim Shamp "Was Second Transplant a Waste of Organs?" *Herald-Sun*, March 2, 2003.

Gilbert Meilaender	"Gifts of the Body," *New Atlantis*, Summer 2006.
Eric M. Meslin	"Organ Transplantation and Medical Ethics," *Sound Medicine*, March 1, 2003.
Robert A. Montgomery	"Insider Trading," *Forbes*, March 27, 2006.
Joseph E. Murray and Anthony L. Komaroff	"The Man Who Lost His Face: How a Severely Burned World War II Pilot with a Will to Live Helped Launch the Age of Organ Transplants," *Newsweek*, December 12, 2005.
Carol M. Ostrom	"The Search for Organ Donors: How Far Is Too Far?" *Seattle Times*, March 21, 2004.
The Economist	"Psst, Wanna Buy a Kidney? Organ Transplants," *The Economist*, November 18, 2006.
Elizabeth Svoboda	"2021: You'll Grow a New Heart," *Popular Science*, June 2006.
Shankar Vedantam	"U.S. Citizens Get More Organs than They Give," *Washington Post*, March 3, 2003.
The Economist	"Your Part or Mine? Organ Transplants." November 18, 2006.

Web sites

Gift of a Lifetime http://www.organtransplants.org/ This Web site, sponsored by a large group of business and medical organizations, aims to educate about the human face of organ transplantation by presenting stories of individuals and families whose lives have been touched by organ transplantation.

Medline Plus http://medlineplus.gov/ This Web site is an educational tool of the National Library of Medicine. Searches on topics such as kidney transplant, heart transplant, liver transplant, and organ donation connect to a large database, providing links to many reliable resources on scientific and medical aspects of organ transplantation.

Organdonor.gov http://www.organdonor.gov/ This is the official U.S. Government Web site for organ and tissue donation and transplantation. It is maintained by the Health Resources and Services Administration (HRSA). Healthcare Systems Bureau (HSB), Division of Transplantation, an agency of the U.S. Department of Health and Human Services. The Web site includes basic information about reducing the risk of organ failure and why organ transplantation is sometimes necessary. Information is also provided about transplantation procedures and about becoming an organ donor.

Organ Keeper PO Box 4413, Middletown, RI 02842 Web site: www.organkeeper.com/ Organ Keeper believes the government's organ donation policies have created an organ donor shortage. It promotes market-based alternatives to the current system of procuring and allocating human organs for transplantation.

Index